MY MON

By Janet Bernhard

Edited by Bob Hadwen

Front Cover Picture by Janet Bernhard

First published in the United Kingdom in 2019 by
Bob Hadwen
at
47 Oakleigh Park Drive
Leigh-on-Sea
Essex SS9 1RP

© 2017 / 2018 Janet Bernhard & Bob Hadwen

ISBN 978 0 900828 95 9

Printed in Great Britain by:
BookPrintingUK, Peterborough, PE2 9BF

MY MOMENTS IN TIME

Introduction by Janet
Message from the Family

1   The War Years
2   No War, New Life
3   More Family Life
4   New Experiences
5   God's Guidance
6   Steps to a New Future
7   To Colombia
8   Early Days in Colombia
9   Expanding the Family
10 Fulfilling Government Regulations
11 Extending Our Territory
12 Troubled Years
13 Returning to Colombia
14 Building a New Church
15 Forgiveness
16 Conclusions

Editor's Note

Introduction by Janet

Originally my intention and desire was to leave an account for my grandchildren of what my life has been like and why I have lived in Colombia. But gradually, as I received help from various people, I was encouraged to go further and publish in book form.

My desire is that through the pages, those who read it will find help and encouragement and a desire to carry on with the Lord's help - just as He has helped me.

Janet

Message from the family

The completion of this book was Mom's wish. It provides a lovely memory of our mother, and her life in England, Switzerland and Colombia – the country she came to love, and which became our home.

This book represents an interesting account of her life, between the joys and struggles of a family seeking to serve the Lord in another country. It brings back many happy memories as well as sad times.

We will be forever grateful as a family with Bob Hadwen for assisting and revising this book to be read in English.

Mom always said we should go step by step in life and have our Lord guide us. There were many times when she found it tough to combine being a full time Missionary in country that was under a constant Guerrilla attack and raising four children in a country in which she did not speak the language, not to mention understand the culture and traditions - living in such a different culture to what she had known as a young girl.

We are thankful for a kind and loving Mother who always wanted the best for us, whose trust in God was unquestionable and who sought to serve Him in all that she did. Her witness to God's involvement and goodness shone through in her life and is evident throughout this book. Even in the dark days, she still had the firm foundation of her faith in our Savior.

Whether you knew Janet (Mom) personally or not, we hope that you will be blessed and challenged by this book – her life.

We hope you will enjoy this book - her life, her blessings as a Missionary, as well as her struggles, the people she touched and blessed - and ultimately, that you can, as well, feel the need to be closer to our Lord.

In loving memory.
Janet Bernhard Spillett 1939 - 2017

Her Children,
Sami, Miriam, Martha & Suzanne

Chapter 1 – The War Years

I realise that preparation for my life ahead began when I was born in London in 1939, only a month after the 2nd World War began in Europe. I arrived into a world at war, with bombs dropping, anxiety, hardship and uncertainty.

These are some of my early memories:

I was born in London, in a hospital in the borough of Clapton, on the 6th of October 1939. The Second World War had begun in September that same year. My first memories were when I was 3 or 4 years old and we lived in Chingford, in an apartment at 26 Rolls Park Avenue. The war was just beginning but the bombing of London was at its worst in 1941-1942.

For me the memories of the war were not as negative as one might believe. This was because my parents approached this with wisdom and tried to make me feel that it was fun (if you can say this!) The reason for this was because an iron shelter was installed and went under the table. Inside were cushions to sit on. I had some books and things and it was playtime with Mum and Dad, a flask of tea and maybe a story from my Dad.

The air raids by the Germans were mostly at night so we often passed a lot time in our shelter. Later the government gave each house a refuge which was built in the garden. These were called Anderson shelters. They were larger and, for me, ours became my "playhouse". I had my toys, and Mum and Dad had their tea. Tea became the comfort drink for the British people during the war. When the siren went it was time to go to the shelter until the "all-clear" went to let the people know it was safe to come out again. At the end of an air-raid the first thing we did was to put the kettle on for a cup of tea. Also at this time we were allocated gas masks - awful objects which frightened me if I had to put one on. It encased your face but allowed you to breath. These were issued in case gas bombs were dropped.

When an air raid occurred the siren would go and we would run to our shelter. You waited for the planes to pass over, and then a dreadful noise started - that was a bomb being dropped. It had a terrible sound and we counted - when it got to ten it stopped and we waited. Then came the explosion and you never knew where the bomb had dropped until the siren went telling us we could now come out of the shelter and we could look to see where the smoke was coming from. It was terrifying and our emotions were mixed because we were glad it wasn't us, but we were sad for those who had suffered.

In those days the radio was our communication with the country and the world. This was when Winston Churchill, our Prime Minister, would encourage the country with his famous speeches. There were many restrictions at this time. Before the lights were switched on in the house the windows were covered in black cloth so that no light from inside could be seen outside. This was so that a town could not be detected from the air. Also there were no street lights. All street and town names were taken down. The idea was that if the country was invaded the enemy had no idea where they were - this sounds ridiculous today.

The war years were not at all easy for many different reasons. One was that a lot of items were rationed and each person had their ration book with coupons. Things like sugar, butter, meat, milk, clothes, and shoes, plus many other items were purchased with coupons. It was customary to give some coupons as a birthday or wedding gift.

A special Sunday tea-time treat could be a slice of bread very thinly cut and with a little bit of precious butter and on top a small amount of sugar. A banana was very rare, because anything that was imported was very costly.

Here are some of my childhood memories:

During the war the government decided to evacuate the children from London out to the countryside away from the bombs and destruction. Generally the children went without their parents but with a school teacher. My sister was disabled. She was born in London when a bomb fell on the hospital just as my mother was giving birth. The nurses passed my Mother onto a trolley and my sister received a bang on the head in the process which affected her brain. Because of those circumstances I was allowed to go with my mother and sister to Wales. We went by train and the journey went on forever - it lasted all day. There was no seat for my Mother and she stood all the way with my sister in her arms. Kathleen was 3 months old at the time.

We were allocated a cottage in the country, in the Rhydol Valley at Devil's Bridge near Aberystwyth. The place was very old – it had no running water in the house, no electricity and no inside toilet. The toilet was in the garden in a shed beside the cottage. There was a wooden bench with a hole in the middle and a bucket underneath. Our toilet paper was newspaper. Sitting there one day I had the fright of my life. Outside, eating our grass, was the biggest deer I had ever seen, with enormous antlers! I was panic stricken and I thought I would have to stay there for the rest of my life, but the animal eventually left for other pastures and I was free once more.

I also remember that one spring-time I had another fright. Outside of our little house, across the road was a stream and normally it flowed gently along, but in spring-time when the snow melted, it became a rushing torrent. My mother collected branches and wood for the wood-burning stove where she cooked our meals. One day she was standing too near the edge and I saw her fall into this torrent of water and she was carried away. I was terrified. I was 4 years old, my baby sister was in the house and we were alone. And then I saw two men carrying my Mother along the road to our house. I thought she was dead. They took her into the kitchen and later I was able to go in and see her. We were thankful she lived to tell the tale.

We lived in that little house for about a year or more. While we were there in Wales we met a Pastor, Pastor Darashar, and his family, from India. His son, Peter, who was about my age, became my friend, and his father taught me choruses. My mother kept in contact with them for many years. In the village nearby there was a little country school and I went there but couldn't understand anything because it was all in Welsh.

My father had to stay in London when we were in Wales. He did not qualify for the army because he had been ill and had trouble breathing, so he had to be an air-raid warden. These brave men were the first on the scene after an air raid, helping people from the bombed out buildings, giving first aid. Also during this time he had to be a milkman (because his factory had closed), and because of this he seldom came to visit us.

His visits were always a surprise because there was no telephone and no mail service so he could not let us know he was coming until he stood there on the door-step. We never knew if he was dead or alive, nor where he was, but it was so special when he came. I remember being so proud when, on one of these visits, I could show him that I had learnt how to tie own my shoes laces - what an achievement!

It is interesting how the memory can store up different times and circumstances in one's life and from that time in Wales I remember the garden and the house. We had no electricity but used candles - I still enjoy the warmth and cosiness that candles can bring. The garden gave us fruit and vegetables too. We were very fortunate because those who lived in the cities and towns could not enjoy all that we had in that little house and its garden.

Now and then we could go into town. A bus passed by our door once a week to Aberystwyth, a town by the sea. We would do the shopping and then enjoy the beach until the bus took us back home in the afternoon. We had no restaurant meals but sandwiches which we brought with us. Lovely memories and of course no bomb scares at that time.

In 1945, when the war ended, we went back to Chingford. I was now 6 years old. Celebrations were held and there was such a relief that it was all over. People could begin to put their lives back into place again. We had a big party in the street and the children wore fancy dress. I longed to be a fairy or a princess but there was no money to buy such clothes - everything was still rationed. So my Aunty Phyllis, who lived with us, remade her nurse's uniform for me - I hated it! In the photo taken to commemorate this party, my face is showing my dislike. All the neighbours donated coupons for the feast. Everyone lent a table and the chairs too. We all worked together and the war produced a wonderful spirit of solidarity. We were one big family.

We were very fortunate in my family because we lost no-one. Many families lost fathers and sons, and other members of the family too. Also our homes were kept safe too. Many people lost everything. There were bombed out houses everywhere. London was a sad sight. In our road a German plane crashed landed and the neighbours almost lynched the pilot. He was taken to a prisoner-of-war camp, so I was told. Now that the war was over our family experienced many changes, and we moved to Walthamstow.

Chapter 2 - No war, new life

It is difficult to know where to begin. When we moved to Walthamstow we went to live with my grandmother Warby, so that she could be looked after. The house was small. There was the front room, where my grandmother lived, and the kitchen; then the washhouse, and beyond that a toilet. Upstairs there were two bedrooms and a small store room. We had a fireplace in the bedroom as there was no other form of heating. Also, in the dining room/kitchen there was a fireplace which had to be polished with blacking. Out in the washhouse my mother did the washing in a boiler, which had an open fire below it to heat the water. Washing flakes and a bit of blue dye made the washing white. Monday was always washing day - come snow, hail or sunshine, without fail, Monday she did the washing. A line was hung in the garden from one end to the other and out went the washing.

My father worked hard making the place more comfortable and he made several improvements. One night while I was in bed my parents broke up the cement boiler in the washhouse and great changes took place - an electric washing machine arrived. A bath was installed, also a hand basin and a proper toilet too - what utter luxury! A big change was in our bath night. Before the new tub came our Saturday bath night was a wonderful ritual. A big galvanised tub was taken down from the hook in the garden and placed in front of the fireplace in the kitchen. Hot water was boiled on the cooker. Our clean nightdresses for the coming week were placed on the fireguard to warm. My sister was first in and she had the smallest amount of water then came my turn and a bit more water went in. While I sat in the soapy water (probably a long while to get the week's dirt off!) my dad read us a story. Yes, we only had a bath on Saturday nights, or on some really special occasion. Those times were so special. Before we went to bed my dad always read us a Bible story. He really loved the Lord.

Not everyone even had a bath at home. One of my school friends told me what happened once when she went with a friend to the local public baths. With your money you paid for a bathroom and the water taps were controlled from outside by an attendant. If the water got cold you could shout to this lady and she would top up the water. But this naughty girl started to call for cold water in a cubicle with another number. All of a sudden a woman shouted, "No, I don't want cold water". The attendant soon worked out what was going on and this girl was banned from the baths for two weeks.

Life outside our house was so interesting. There was a constant flow of people selling things from carts or wheelbarrows and some with a horse and cart. The bread, milk and coal all came by horse and cart. Others collected rags and bones, and then there was the man who collected tin and iron. The fishmonger came on Saturday. The horses of course left their excrement and my dad paid me 3 pence to collect a bucketful for the garden. This was great fun until my friends laughed at me when I was much older, and that source of income was then abandoned. Near to our house the bakers had stables and a smithy for the horses' shoes to be changed. I loved going there - I can still recall the smell of the burning hooves.

We had no television at that time but the radio was a wonderful instrument which kept us spellbound for hours. Every day at 4 pm was "Children's Hour". The story of Dick Barton, a series, was one of my favourites. But another series was read to us on the radio from the book "Heidi", by Johanna Spyri - that really took my imagination. The first time I saw television was at a neighbour's house in 1953 when Queen Elizabeth II was crowned.

However, Saturday morning pictures beat the lot. We would go in a group from our street and met on the street corner first. We were very happy to be away for a while and no doubt our parents were also glad for the break. Roy Rogers, Black Beauty, the Three Musketeers, Laurel and Hardy, Charley Chaplin and many others kept us laughing and shouting for a couple of hours. Sometimes my mum would give me a few pennies to buy some half-price stale cakes from the bakers on our way to the picture house, or cinema. That was a special treat.

The Games we played

Life was fun in those days and we played out in the street in summer until it changed to autumn and the days grew shorter and the light faded early. After doing my chores in the house I would ask if I could go 'out to play', and my friends and I would meet on the corner and decide what we were going to do. Sometimes we would invent dramas or plays and make up the story, work out our parts and what we would wear. Usually by then it was time to go home because it was late. There was one lady in the street that had some wonderful dresses in a trunk and once she let us dress up for one of our performances. One house had a row of steps going up to the front door. These were our gallery for the audience.

When we had no money for the Saturday morning pictures we would make what we called a grotto. We would find some earth or sand, pick flowers and leaves, find some stones and make a picture and ask people passing if they wanted to have a look and we would charge them. A few paid up!

A few years on we enjoyed "kiss chase". The boys would hide and the girls would go looking for them. If you found a boy you could kiss him. Goodness me, all this was so innocent at the time! Another super game was going to another street and knocking on a door and running for your life. Our days were very peaceful and easy going. We went to the park together and played there until it was time to go home. We were always on our own, no grown up ever had to come with us for protection. We had very few toys - I had a doll made from my grandma's old stockings, and I loved it. Later my Aunty Joan gave me a real doll, her body was made from cloth but her head was porcelain. The only problem was that she was top heavy and would fall forward and bash you on the head. One day my sister had this sad experience and in her rage threw the doll to the ground. Goodbye Joanie!

Christmas time and the Presents

Our Christmases had their particular traditions. On the 24th of December we had a stocking or the biggest sock you could find and this was placed at the foot of the bed. Father Christmas would come at night, and in the morning, very early, we would find our sock full of special things.

On Christmas Eve I would go with my mother to visit my aunt, uncle and cousin John and we would have hot mince pies and give our presents to them. Later, when I was older, I went carol singing with the young people from our church. This was such a special time. We would visit someone from the church, maybe one who had been ill or was very old, and we sang outside their door. Sometimes we were invited in to the home and they would give us hot chocolate and mince pies.

One Christmas the Sunday school put on a Christmas play. Of all things they made me an angel! My Uncle Len made me some wings but they were of plaster of Paris and the weight nearly killed me - I was a fallen angel!

On Christmas morning we went to church. The sermon always seemed so long - maybe because we could only open our big present when we arrived home and had finished Christmas dinner. After the war things were very scarce for some time and we made do with homemade gifts. I longed for a dolls house and a two wheeled bicycle. Once I asked my dad to talk to Father Christmas and ask him if he could get me a dolls house.

One Christmas, to my great surprise Father Christmas actually came to our house. He came down the stairs, traditionally he was said to come down the chimney, and I couldn't understand why he did not come down the kitchen chimney which was bigger. And why did he have my Dad's slippers on? When he had given me my presents, I insisted on accompanying him so I could see how he went up that tiny chimney. Somehow he convinced me to stay downstairs, but that night I kept myself awake until Father Christmas came - Father Christmas did not get much sleep that night either. Next day my dad told me that Father Christmas was for small children and now that I was bigger I could be told who Father Christmas was and one day I would have my dolls house. I felt pleased that I was now big enough to understand and my imagination and fantasy about Father Christmas ended happily.

My Dad's promise, that one day I would have a dolls house, came the next year. A friend at work told him that his daughter no longer wanted her dolls house. Somehow my dad brought it home and hid it in his shed where he did all his carpentry. When I was in bed at night my parents spent hours remodelling that house. It had curtains, carpets, furniture, lamps, and tiny dolls, a bedroom, living room, kitchen and a bathroom - it was a dream. My dad enjoyed making it so much he hardly let me play with it and the same with the little bed he made for my dolls.

That Christmas I learnt a lesson in patience. Sometimes we have to wait a long time for something we want but in time the best comes along. My Dad would tell me, "When I can I will." My dear Dad taught me many such lessons.

The other longing was for a bicycle. It seemed that everyone else had one but not me. My friends would let me have a turn on theirs to go up and down the street but they always took so long before my turn came. One Christmas my Dad took me outside and proudly presented me with the longed-for bicycle. But, horror of horrors, it was so antique! It was like the ones in my grandma's picture album. I was so embarrassed I did not want to take it out to the street. Somehow he understood and much later changed it for a more modern one. What a special dad he was.

With the new modern bike we used to go out on Saturdays to Epping Forrest and take cheese rolls and something to drink with us. There was very little traffic on the roads and we would go for miles. My mum would have a gorgeous meal ready for when we arrived home. We enjoyed this sitting round the table together.

Greenleaf Road Baptist Church

Another very important part of my life was spent at the church. It was near our house and my family all went there. My grandad was moderator during the war when the Pastor went into the army as a Chaplin. [A moderator someone who is appointed to look after a church when there is no minister]

My Uncle Hubert and his wife Vi, with their children, Margaret and Tony, were Baptist missionaries and went to China. My Aunty Hilda was a Sunday school teacher and all my cousins also went there. Many people in that church helped form and transform my character. I was not an easy child. I loved to make people laugh but often at the wrong times. However, I owe so much to the patience of those teachers and leaders. Miss Sayer, Silvia Cowlan who was our Girls Brigade leader, Joan

Freestone our Captain, Edna Blackburn, all of these and very many more - thank you.

I have so many wonderful memories of my days at the church. My dad was Sunday school superintendent and once a year we were taken to the seaside at Southend–on-Sea on the train. This was well organised because several other churches went too. We got on at Walthamstow but at the next station down the line another group joined us and so on until the train was full. It was so exciting. We took our lunch with us - some sandwiches, probably jam, but we ate them well before lunchtime. When at last we arrived at our destination we were taken to a section of the beach to play and bath our feet in the sea. That is if the tide was in. Some of my friends were given a few pence and we went to the amusement machines which had a crane and if you were very lucky you could pick up some useless article. At the end of the day we reunited with the other groups and went back to the station. I think we mostly slept all the way home, but we talked about next year and looked forward to the next outing. For most of us it was the only time we went to the seaside or had a day out.

One of my friends, Jill Owen, had polio when she was small and she had to wear a leg iron. I was so surprised when we went on one of these outings and she took off the iron and, with her sister Anne, managed to get to the sea to bath her feet. She always impressed me because she never complained or let it hinder her. Our friendship has lasted down the years with most of that group and I am grateful for such special friends - Wendy Heath, Maureen Patmore, Doreen Childs, Marion Lefever, Brenda Green and Anne and Jill Owen, plus many others too. On these outings we were always together and in the Girls Brigade and Christian Endeavour.

What glorious years those were and they formed our character and Christian principles. But it must have been hard work for our leaders.

Once a year those over 11 years old were taken camping to the Isle of Wight. We went with the Girls Life Brigade and we camped out in tents for about a week. This was held at a camp site run by a Mr and Mrs Baisley. They were very kind people who also made the best porridge I have ever eaten!

We had tent inspection every morning and the leader would come round to check that all was neat and tidy and that we had had a wash. Of course there were rules which had to be broken. No food in the tent - so we had a magnificent midnight party when we got out all our secret food. No torches at night, no leaving the campsite at night - once my friends and I escaped into the park supposedly to meet the local boys who did not turn up but we had a round on the swings and crept back. We were not detected! We had lots of outings and games in groups too. It was wonderful. On the last night before returning home there was a bonfire and sausages to cook over the fire.

Another activity in the church was Christian Endeavour. This was a weekly meeting from 6-7pm. Each month for four weeks there was a special theme. One week we were ship wrecked and so we sat on the floor, no song books, no bibles, all had to be done from memory, imagining that we were on a desert island and we had lost everything. This was very good because it helped us to memorise verses from the bible and the songs too. Another week we wrote to missionaries and also read out the replies to the letters we had received. Each week was different but those meetings prepared me so much for my future ministry. I learnt how to speak in public and to have confidence. We memorised scripture verses and also we were taught to be aware of the needs of other people and how to evangelise. The Bible was taught and we learnt how to find the books, chapters and verses as well as memorised portions of the Bible. This training was so valuable for my future. I owe so much to my leaders of those days and their patience with me.

My circle of friends was quite small, but we saw each other every day. We went to the same school, the same church and we all lived near each other too. We went to the same school until the 11 plus exam - that divided the brains from the not so bright ones. Guess which group I was in! I hated school and I think I began my education when I left there. You could not get any lower in the list of achievements than I did. My name was never in the first 10 who passed the exams very well. One year my name was second to last, as I pointed out to my poor Dad, but he said the teacher told him that the last one was ill and did not even sit the exams! He was not fooled!

It was sport I loved, especially swimming. When I learnt to swim, I think my Dad was not sure if, at first, I really could swim. He thought I had one foot on the bottom. So one day he said if I could swim the length of the baths, that included the deep end, he would buy me a handbag. To his surprise he had to buy me one!

I took to the water like a fish and soon was winning competitions in my class and then in my school. Later I swam for the county and amazingly went for the trials to represent England in the Olympics. That was as far as I got but it did my low self-esteem such a lot of good. While preparing me for competitions I had a very strict trainer and I went to the local swimming pool every day except Sunday. I had to swim up and down the lanes for an hour and return in the evening again for the same. I loved it.

When I began training for the county I was told I had to have a regulation swim suit which was very expensive, so my dear Mum decided to knit me one. So far so good - except when I climbed out of the water the wretched thing started to drop and stretch - I managed to pull it up and regain my dignity! My trainer managed to get me two regulation suits later - what a relief.

I went to William McGuffie Secondary School after the eleven plus exam. This school had the nick-name William McScruffy. We were a rough bunch, but our class teacher was the worst, I reckon. He used to throw chalk at us, and we would duck behind the desk lid. Our lessons were the dullest you could get - we spent hours just copying from a text book into an exercise book. We had ink wells and pens with a scratchy nib. I remember the first days of the new school year when we were given new exercise books and I would begin a new page with such good intentions, but it was so sad when the first blotch of ink fell on the page and it was spoilt.

We once went to a museum - that was also boring but next day was worse when we had to write in those books about the school trip. Also, on the first day back at school after the summer holidays we had to report our activities. I often spent my summer holidays on the farm in Writtle where my Aunty Joan and Uncle Wally worked. Well, I thought they owned it but, never mind, what innocence we have when young. Those long golden days were so wonderful. I can't ever remember it raining, but of course it must have done. Their house was so old, there was no electricity and at night we had candle light. There was fresh milk from the farm, homemade bread, also jam and butter - all homemade. I really loved it there. My Dad wrote me letters with drawings on each page. I learnt to drive the tractor and help with the hay making.

One day we learnt that an old lady from a house down the road had died and the house was emptied for new people to move in, and we found out that some things had been thrown out. The next day, with a friend, we went exploring to see what there was for us. What bounty! There were long dresses, handbags, leather gloves, make-up, purses, scarves, hankies, shoes, and hats with feathers and flowers. We took as much as we could carry and spent our free time dressing up in all that finery. Our imagination took us into ballrooms, handsome young men, dances; we thought we had become "Dames of Society".

I always arrived back in London brown as a berry, maybe with some dirt added. No-one checked if we washed or not. On my return, of course, it was back to school again, but at least I had something interesting to write about. It seemed to me that summers those years back were hot and wonderful, but they had their difficulties too. We had no refrigerator, just a slab of marble in the pantry. There was no plastic so when you went to the shop for bread or fruit, or whatever, everything was put into paper bags.

For several years after the war we had to use the coupons in our ration books and certain goods were in short supply. A Baptist church in America supported our family and we received parcels from them, and many others also received them too. Those cardboard boxes contained so many wonderful surprises. There were tins of peaches and fruit, cake mixes, biscuits, and also some toys and clothing. I remember one in particular because I came home from school one day and my mother had unpacked the box and put the things in the living room window like a shop. And there, hanging up, was a really lovely party dress for me. It had a skirt of fine material in different colours - lilac, pink and pale blue. I loved it. I am not sure how many boxes came but each one was a wonderful surprise.

Then one day a letter came to tell us that the lady who sent the boxes was coming to England and would like to visit us. My Mother was very nervous and cleaned the house from top to bottom. She made cakes and sandwiches using up the precious things from a box. On top of that we had to have a bath in the middle of the week! I was allowed to miss school that afternoon, what joy! The lady arrived and announced that she did not have very much time, so my Mum made the tea and we sat down. The lady drank her tea, thanked us and left. Of course she did not notice that the beds had clean sheets, the floor was spotless and even less that we had bathed mid-week! But when she had gone we sat down again and really enjoyed our tea-time. All we had had time for was to thank her for the boxes and her generosity and she was gone again. So much fuss for so short a visit.

Chapter 3 – More Family Life

Those days after the war we had very few holidays and we had never been away from home and slept in a hotel. Sometimes we had a day out to somewhere nearby. Then one day my Dad announced that Kath, my sister was going to stay with an aunt and uncle and we were going to Faversham to stay a few days with my Aunt Floss and Uncle Jim. In this town the family Spillett was well known and our ancestors came from there. Those dear people were so kind to us. They lived in a tiny house but made room for us. There was a basement under the house where the vegetables were stored because it was very cold down there, but I remember it had such a marvellous smell. Each day we went to the seaside by train and Aunt Floss made us jam sandwiches to take with us. I am sure they were made with much love but the first day we did not eat all of them and took them back with us in the evening. For our tea the sandwiches appeared once more, even dryer than before!

Next day the ducks on a pond were given our dry sandwiches and my Dad bought us a lunch instead. We were so grateful for the few days of fun we had together and I met lots of aunts and uncles I had never seen before. My grandad Spillett was born in that town and my forefathers are mentioned in the town's archives as far back as 1664. The family were serving the Lord far back in history and we found information about them which told us that there had been Pastors and Christians in the Spillett family. One day my Dad decided we would take a walk round the local cemetery and there to his horror he found his name on a tomb stone - William Alan Spillett - he did not want to stay long, that was very eerie!

I have always been very proud of our family history and there is a road named after us there called "Spillett Lane". It is interesting how from generation to generation there have been people who have served the

Lord. My Uncle Hubert and his wife Violet were missionaries in China, and in Walthamstow so many of my aunts and uncles served in the church.

Once at school, on one of those boring days, we had to write an essay about what we wanted to be when we grew up. Well my uncle and aunt had recently come back from China and one day I sat beside my aunt and she had a beautiful Chinese dress on made of silk. I loved it. So I wrote in my exercise book that I wanted to be a missionary. I thought that would be very exciting and I could wear lovely dresses. What an illusion! But at least no-one else in my class had the same idea.

Holiday time was always very special for us because it was the only time in the year when we could get some time to ourselves without my sister being with us. Living with Kath was very tense because of her disabilities. She did not understand us nor could she communicate with us meaningfully and she was probably very frustrated and showed it in her uncontrolled rage. But we often went away with my parent's friends George and Lily Lefever and Marion, their daughter - she and I were like cousins. I was always pleased when Marion had new clothes because I would then get the dresses she no longer needed.

I believe the only time my Dad had any money was when the firm paid him in advance for his holiday. Once he came home from work and it was the beginning of his holidays, we were in the kitchen and with these pound notes he threw them in the air and called out '"look I am rich". We rushed to catch a few, laughing. Our favourite places for our holidays were in Margate or Broadstairs and later a friend from work loaned us his holiday chalet in Pevensey Bay. They were golden days.

***

My Father's Employment

Before the war my father worked as a carpenter and went from sweeping up the sawdust to being the timber buyer for the firm. At first it was called Haggis's then later the name changed to Pollard's. This firm was appointed to do repairs for the Queen. They also made Steinway pianos. During the war a bomb damaged part of a corner of the House of Lords and my grandfather, William Spillett, carved a part of one of those famous chairs, which are like thrones, to repair it.

My father was not far behind. One day he arrived home from work and casually said, "Oh today I was in Buckingham Palace". The firm was called in to make a showcase for the first year's clothes of Prince Charles. This apparently was the custom. So my Dad went to inspect the case and type of timber used for the showcase of the Queen's first baby clothes. Then he had the task of finding the exact timber and buying it before the case was made by the carpenters. When it was finished my Dad was sent to Buckingham Palace again to make sure it was correct.

Also, to celebrate the Festival year [1951 – the Festival of Britain], the government built a concert hall on the Thames embankment called "The Royal Festival Hall". For that, too, my Dad bought the timber, and the firm was responsible for all the woodwork inside the hall.

With good reason I am very proud of my Dad and all he achieved in his lifetime. He taught me so much in values and honesty. He showed his love for the Lord with his lifestyle, and he was faithful both at work and at home.

My Mother also had her share of fame. She worked for a firm called "Britains" - they sold toy soldiers and farm animals, etc., which were made of lead. She was the one who painted the sample pieces for display. After the war she did her work from home, painting hundreds of these toys every week in a corner of our kitchen. They were brought to her and collected weekly.

Now I will tell you something about my sister Kathleen. Kathleen Mary was born in June 1942, in the Salvation Army hospital in London. Unfortunately she started to arrive just as an air-raid began, and the nurses had to put my mother on a trolley and rush her outside. We understood that my sister was delivered by the side of the road and she somehow received a bang on her head which resulted in cerebral palsy..

Life was very difficult for all of us. Kathleen could not walk properly or talk coherently, she was never able to read or write, or take care of her own needs or even dress herself. She lived in a world of her own and I believe she was very frustrated. If we laughed and she did not know why then she would have a terrible tantrum and scratch herself or anyone near at hand. She went to day care after a while but learnt some terrible words there. One day our Pastor came to visit and for some unknown reason Kath took a dislike to him and came out with the worst of her swear words. We were of course so embarrassed but, dear man, he took it well - I imagine he had a good laugh with his family when he arrived home.

Life was a constant state of tension among us and my poor Mother sometimes took her frustration out on me, which of course I found very unjust. Once a week it was my turn to take Kath to the local park in her pram, which was huge and very ugly. Today she would have had a wheelchair. I remember one occasion when she wanted to go up the slide, which I remember was very high. If she did not get her own way she had a tantrum and this would sometimes mean she was sitting on the floor screaming. So I took her to the slide. We were half way up and she would not go up or down. Maybe you can imagine, the children behind me shouting to move on and Kath determined not to, and her vocabulary at full blast. I think the sheer horror of that incident was so painful I have no memory of how we moved her one way or the other but never again did I let her go up the slide.

Living with Kath taught me many things and one area was to be more understanding with people who have disabilities like Kath. People can be very unkind in giving their opinion but often it is because they do not understand. I found it so difficult when out with her and if she had a tantrum people made comments like, "she is too spoilt", or "if that were my child I would spank her". For me it was sometimes difficult to manage my emotions. I swung between feeling sorry for her and being cross with her. As a family we lived in tension most of the time. As she grew up it became increasingly difficult to look after her, and gradually it became clear something had to be done about this. My parents had to face the difficult decision of her going to live away from home. This must have been very difficult for my mother, but when Kath was 13 years old she went to live in a home which had house parents, with a group of people who shared her problems. Although difficult at first, it was also a relief for us all and Kath was very happy. In fact she never wanted to come home again, not even for a day.

Life took on a complete change for all of us. I was 15 and somewhat independent and rebellious, and with this attitude my Mother suddenly realised she had another daughter to give her attention to. But I did not want that. One day, in my anger, she sent me to my room. Outside my window was a roof leading down into the garden and I climbed out and went to my grandad, telling him that Mum and Dad knew I was there. My Dad came looking for me later and took me back home again and I was in more trouble than before.

I went through a lot of teenage rebellion, and confess I was very unkind to my Mum, for which some years later I asked her to forgive me, and of course she did. We began to realise that we were now a family which could function better, and there were changes, and we had some very lovely surprises. My Dad had his annual holiday but there was no money to be able to go away together. We were sitting in the kitchen and we heard something drop through the letter box. It was an envelope with money in it and a note that said: "Have a happy holiday"!

And we did! We went to Broadstairs and stayed in a hotel. I believe my parents fell in love again on that holiday, they certainly were much happier than ever I could remember. We never found out who that generous person was who gave us that holiday.

Kathleen never came home again, and we began to learn to live a normal family life.

On Sundays we went to tea with grandad William and grandma Rose (Spillett). My grandad was so special to me. He was a big man, and he smoked a pipe. He loved doing puzzles, and he had a big green leather chair. I would sit on his lap and he would tell me stories. He had a lovely chiming clock and the sound of that clock was very comforting.

Many articles were still rationed for a time after the war so when we went to tea we had to ask one of my grandparents to give us some butter or jam, or we took our own. Grandad had a shed at the bottom of the garden which was his work room too. It had a wonderful smell of wood shavings. He loved classical music and in summer, when he had the door open, the music would drift down the garden and could be heard in the house. I have so many lovely memories of my dear grandad and grandma.

Christmas at their home was so wonderful. We used to dress up in my grandma's clothes and do dramas invented by my grandad. We also had our presents from the rest of the family at those parties. One year my Dad received some hair gel which he did not like, so he saved it and next year he gave it to an uncle of mine. Strangely enough the hair gel came back to my Dad one year, and so he decided to uncover the mystery. How we all laughed about that gift that went round to four uncles.

I could tell grandad Spillett anything and he was my confidant and helper. Every Tuesday there was a prayer meeting in the church and he and my Aunty Hilda used to come to us for a cup of tea before going home. I could wait up in my pyjamas on Tuesdays for him to pray with me and then I was off to bed.

One Tuesday, as usual, he prayed with me and I went to bed. Downstairs they were talking and then noticed that grandad was asleep but, no, he had died. Peacefully he had gone to be with the Lord he so loved. Next day came the shock - grandad had gone to be with Jesus. He had been placed in the front room and the undertaker, Mr White or Mr Black (I cannot remember now!) came with the coffin. As our house was very small they had to stand it on end. I cried thinking that his knees were hurt as they tried to get out of the house. Christmas was never the same again and we missed him so much. Grandma Rose died some years later and eventually we went to live in that same house. It was so full of happy memories. It was called "Davington" - 102, Nelson Road, Chingford, London.

My grandparents from my mothers' side were Mr and Mrs Warby - I always called them "Nanna" and "Grandpa". I don't have many memories of grandpa because he died when I was very small, but I knew that he made wooden jewellery boxes, all shapes and sizes, with tiny hinges and fasteners. He also played the violin and loved classical music.

Well, my Mother inherited the violin and she imagined me as a violin player, but that was never to be! I hated the thing. My classmates were into guitars and there was I trudging this violin back and forward to music classes. I was so embarrassed. Thankfully, my Mother accepted the reality soon enough.

My Nanna Warby was old when we went to live with her in Walthamstow. I was about 6 or 7 at the time, but I remember that she made me a lovely doll out of old woollen stockings - it was soft and cuddly. She stayed in bed mostly and when I was ill and home from school she would get out her picture postcard collection and the photo albums and she would tell me a story about them all. With the chimney alight and the room cosy I remember how I felt protected and loved. In her last times before she died she was in an old people's home but happy and well looked after.

When she died her furniture and belongings were sorted out between my aunts and uncles, all except the old organ which my Nanna had in her room. It was so eaten up with woodworm my Dad had to have it taken away. We lived in that house where my mother was born for some 20 years - 6 Browns Road, Walthamstow.

Now what did we eat in those days? It was very different from today. The rationing continued for some years after the war and it was quite a time before anything luxurious was available. Our meals were wholesome and basic and, in my memory, always the same every week.

On Sunday we had our famous Roast Beef, when there was meat available. Because Monday was washday, we had Bubble and Squeak, a lovely fry up - this was Sunday's leftovers all mixed together in the frying pan and the greens squeaked when cooking – it was delicious! I can't remember now what came every day but we had vegetables from the garden or the allotment, and my mother made the most wonderful apple pie with custard.

Then there was our famous "fish and chips". It was always wrapped in newspaper, with some vinegar and salt, and for a few pence we could buy the crackling from the batter. We bought winkles from the fishmonger, who came round with a barrow on Saturdays, and with a slice of bread and butter - what memories all this brings back. Sometimes in winter we would put a slice of bread on a toasting fork and sit before the fire and toast the bread. The smell of toasting bread is unique and, with some butter spread onto it, wonderful - the taste was as good as the smell.

For some time during and after the war bananas and oranges were very rare, and a Sunday treat was a piece of bread with a very little butter and some sugar on top. We were never without something to eat, even during wartime when food was often very scarce, and we always sat round the table for our meals. Those times were special; we would share the day's happenings and always prayed to thank the Lord for His provision, which is maybe why we never went without a meal.

Chapter 4 - New experiences

My passion at school was swimming but that was not going to get me a job. It was becoming more and more difficult to find work, so they let me stay on another year at school in the hope that something might turn up. I enjoyed that last year very much. I was named "Head Girl" and with new authority I blossomed. This new position gave me confidence and I went about my duties with my badge pinned on my uniform. I rang the bell at class changes, ran errands for the staff and sometimes I took messages to the headmaster. In short, I don't think I did much school work and, of course, that time soon came to an end and I had to leave school.

I went for an interview at a local florist's. I think the owner was from the church, but I sneezed through most of the interview - hay fever - so that was ruled out as a possibility! I think my poor Dad must have wondered whatever to do with me, but one day my Dad's friend, who worked for the Post Office, suggested I went to have an interview to work as a Telephonist. I had an interview and, amazing as it seemed, I got the job.

I was employed at last. I loved it. I was in Faraday House, near St. Paul's Cathedral. I worked among a row of girls and women and I soon made lots of friends. The job was very interesting and in those days we answered the "0" for the operator and then we connected the call to its destination. In the same room the emergency calls came in and also calls to and from Buckingham Palace, which had its own board where very trustworthy and well trained people worked those lines.

I am not sure how long I worked there, maybe two years, but times changed and it was decided that women should also take the night shifts, which were only done by the men before. As I had to travel by train it was decided that I should leave there and find a job as a receptionist/ telephonist in an office. I went to work for a firm of lawyers in Holborn, which I also enjoyed. There I made friends with a girl in the typing pool and we used to go to concerts or plays together. Once a month we would stay in town and maybe go to the theatre or a concert in the Royal Albert Hall. My love of classical music began in those concerts.

Then my friend and I decided we would go on holiday together. What an adventure! I believe I was about 19 years old at the time. We saved hard and booked to go on a guided tour to Switzerland. While on that holiday we really did have some adventures. One free afternoon we took a pathway following the yellow marks on the trees. We were told these were the official walkways. We found ourselves way up the mountain and on one of the Alps. There was a little hut and two old people sat outside. They called us over and offered us something to drink – maybe goats' milk because there were lots of goats about. We couldn't speak a word of their language but we made it clear we were grateful and made our way down the mountain again. On another free day we went on the train to Interlaken but unfortunately we got on the wrong train on the way back and when we stood up to get off the train at our stop it raced on at a terrible speed - we were on our way to ITALY! We had no extra money with us and no passports. The conductor arrived and we eventually were let off some long way away from the hotel. We arrived back late at night and the tour guide was very cross with us, but when we explained he forgave us.

This holiday was very interesting and opened up a new world for me. Also, at the same time, I was very bored with going to church all the time and I found, contrary to my parents' idea, that people "in the world", as they put it, were not the miserable, unhappy people I was told about. I found that I was the unhappy one in the office on Monday morning and all these people had had such a good time over the weekend. Going to church was more of a tradition than a conviction. It had become a habit – all the family went so I went too. But I was not free to do whatever I wanted. At that time you were under your parents control until you were 21 years old. Then I was given the key to the front door and allowed to stay out until 10pm at night.

When I was 21 I began a friendship with one of the fellows from church - Michael Forrest. We were great friends, and we bought a veteran car and spent many happy hours mending this old Ford. Once we went with two other friends on the London to Brighton veteran car run. What fun that was! Michael and I thought we would marry one day, but my Dad didn't think very much of the idea and he suggested we separate for a time to see what happened. I later lost contact with Michael and didn't meet him again until many, many years later.

I wanted something different in my life. I was very unhappy at home and church. So when my cousin Moira wrote from Denmark, telling me of the great time she was having there, and invited me to go and that she would help me get a job, I decided this was what I was waiting for. It must have been a great shock for my parents but I was determined and one day I set out for Tilbury docks to get on a cargo boat heading for Denmark. Next day we headed out to the North Sea, my adventure had begun. But what awaited me was not exactly what I had imagined.

That night, when we were in the middle of the North Sea, a terrible storm struck us and I was tied to my bunk and listened to the things in the kitchen falling about. My bedroom chair raced first down the room then back again. I really thought my end had come. Another Jonah, but no great fish was provided. I was very scared and wondered if this was the Lord punishing me, but we reached land next day and as we went through the Kiel Canal I felt safer. My cousin was waiting for me at the dock and was so pleased to see I was all in one piece. A warning had gone out on the radio that a ship was in the storm and in difficulties - that was us!

I stayed for a few days with my cousin and she showed me around Copenhagen. I loved it there, but reality hit me on Monday morning when she took me to my job. I was under the illusion that I would work in an office, but of course I had not learnt the language so the only job she could find for me was as a maid. I was to work cleaning the house and looking after three children. Help! I had no experience whatever with children and housework was not on my list of favourite jobs either. What a shock. I had to wear a uniform, one colour for serving at table, and another one for the housework, and the lady of the house rang a bell when she wanted me. I could hardly believe what I was into. There went one big bit of pride.

I was ashamed to admit to my parents that I was working as a maid. Too proud, I told them in my letters home that all was well. My duties consisted of doing the housework, serving at table, and at night answering to any calls from the children. The little girl was teething and I did not get much sleep. Also the cleaning was very hard work. Gone was my idea of meeting some handsome Dane. The only men I saw were the milkman and the postman, both very old, or so they seemed to me. I was very lonely, although I made good friends with the girl who was the cook. She was young and spoke English and we got on well together. She taught me many things, helping me do my job.

One day we were told that the family were going on holiday and in that time we were to spring-clean the whole house. That meant going on hands and knees to scrub the parquet flooring and polish it again. This really was very hard work so when we finished the job before the family came home we decided to give ourselves a treat. We would make a feast, and invite a couple of friends in. We would use the best china, have some wine, buy the best food at the market with the card we were given, and in general have a wonderful time. Our guests came and we had the dining room table full to overflowing when we suddenly heard a car pull up outside the front door - the owner of the house had come home! We were in PANIC! We had to hide the food and the friends. I went to the door and kept him informed how things were, while in the dining room they were rushing around. My cousin was under my bed, the food in the shower, every trace hidden. Fortunately the man never went into the dining room, and left quite soon - he had come back for a suit because he had a surprise business meeting to attend. When he had gone we were so exhausted by their surprise visit I don't think we enjoyed the feast as much as we thought we would. But we did laugh afterwards.

I was not in Denmark for very long. One night my Mother phoned from England to tell me that my Dad was in hospital; he had a thrombosis and was very ill. I should come home at once. But how? During the short time I was in Denmark I had not saved any of my wages but, like the prodigal son, I had spent all I had. I did not know how I could get home. That night I remember I sat on the bed and thought about what I had actually achieved in going to Denmark. I was so sure I could manage my own life and did not need anyone telling me what to do, but actually I was worse off than before. I realised I needed to ask the Lord to forgive me for my rebellious attitude and several other things too. I asked for forgiveness and accepted the Lord as my Saviour. I felt so relieved. A change took place in me that night, and I really wanted to do something worthwhile with my life. My sister did not have that privilege but I did, and from then on my desire to serve the Lord began.

Next day, the lady of the house asked me who had telephoned the night before. A call from England in those days was something very rare. I told her my news about my Father. She said I could go home and she gave me the money to do so. I think she was relieved I was going! A few days later I was on my way home and went straight to the hospital. My Father was so pleased to see me and I told him "Dad, the prodigal daughter has come home" and I explained what had happened. My Dad came home from hospital and he lived eleven years more.

In the following eleven years a lot happened. We were living in my grandfather's house in Chingford, and that brought back so many lovely memories. We were attending Greenleaf Road Baptist Church and I began to help in Sunday school and with the Junior Boys of the Boys Brigade. I loved this new challenge and prepared myself by taking different courses. I was single and had time to spend with these boys. I had to do a course on how to play football and became a real fan of the game! I took them to camp with Edna Blackburn (Sutton) and we made very good friends with a couple who have been faithful all the way since then – John and Mary Buck. In short, I was very happy and I felt that I was achieving something worthwhile.

Well, I have done some very crazy things in life and most of those things have been great fun. I decided I wanted to go on the Thames in a houseboat. So I convinced Wendy Heath (Stout) and some friends from the office to come with me on this adventure. None of us had any experience at guiding a boat up the Thames. We took charge of our new home at Kingston-on-Thames. We were given half an hour's lesson on how to work this great boat and off we set. I think there were six of us.

No-one was prepared for the bridges we had to go under and the fact that part of the deck was higher than the bridge. Panic set in as the bridge got nearer and still we were desperately trying to lower this glass cover. Amazingly someone got us through to the other side in one piece without us hitting the bridge. We laughed so much that first day. We had to learn how to navigate locks where you went in at one level and came out the other side higher up. One day we arrived near to the sea. I am not sure where that was but we tied our boat to the side of the sea wall and went to the pictures. Horror of horrors, when we arrived back a small crowd had gathered by our boat. The tide had gone out and the boat was partly hanging on the side of the wall. The local old seamen gave us plenty of advice on how to tie the boat to the wall and give enough rope for movement. Fortunately no great damage was done, although it was a bit untidy inside.

In 1962 my dad wanted to move and live near the sea. So they went house hunting and ended up in Leigh-on-Sea in Essex. They found a lovely house, not exactly on the sea front but it was a short walk away. Dad and I would meet at Fenchurch Street station after work and come home on the train. We would get off at Leigh and walk along the sea-front and home. These were such special times. Of course, this was when the weather allowed us to walk comfortably. We soon found a church where we felt at home, and we began to attend and get to know many special people there. Leigh Road Baptist Church, with the Pastor and Mrs Nash, became our spiritual home. Dad and I had been very busy in the church in Walthamstow and so we decided to sit back and take it easy for a while. But it seemed that the Lord had other plans and it was not long before we found ourselves "back in action", once more. Rev Nash came to visit and asked my Dad to help in the church as missionary secretary.

Dad had always been very interested in this area, maybe because his brother (Hubert Spillett) had been a missionary in China with the BMS. So dad took on the privilege. He also told me that he asked the Lord to allow him to see ten people go to the mission field during his time as missionary secretary. At that time, we had no idea that one of those ten would be me. So while dad began his ministry to missionaries I was asked to begin the Life Boy section of the Boys Brigade at Leigh Road. I had worked in Life Boys in Walthamstow under the good hand and leadership of Edna Blackburn (Mrs Edna Sutton), and I was now a trained leader after the many different courses I had taken. I was qualified to begin this new venture at Leigh Road.

First of all, a group of helpers were chosen - nine people in all - and I trained them for the first meeting with the young boys, ranging from the age 8 to 11 years old. This was such a special time in my life, I loved the work, and my desire to win every one of these dear boys for the Lord was my goal. With the help of these very special people and the church behind us, the group soon grew and we had up to 25-30 boys. Each year we took them to camp to Romney Bay. What a glorious time we had together: games, water pistol battles, outings on the miniature railway. It was such fun and each day we had our devotional with the boys and many came to know the Lord as Saviour.

In the church at Leigh I came to know so many wonderful people who have been such faithful friends over the years: Dawn and Alan Tucker and their children, as well as Audrey Bowers, and Mary and Paul Lewis. Well if you look through the church directory most of the people have been interested in what I have done. I cannot name everyone and maybe you feel left out, but I am so grateful for the loving care and help I received from so many dear people. David and May Gray, and Den and Vera Batt, who also gave a lot of support, are now with the Lord.

Also in the church a "witness team" was formed by Chris and Margaret Chilvers. We called the team "the Fishermen". There were about ten of us: Ken and Kath Batt, Doreen Alsupp, Joy Sampson, Roger Chilvers - just to name a few. We met during the week for prayer and bible study and on Friday night we went to the coffee bars and discotheques in Southend - which were the dens of iniquity at that time - to speak with people about the Lord. On Friday nights at about 11 o'clock, while we were in these places, there was a group of people meeting at the church to pray for us because sometimes it was quite a dangerous place to be in. My dad was part of that group. Once, a fight broke out and we were caught up in it and not able to get out. One person broke the neck off a bottle to use it as a weapon. I was glad that people were praying for our protection! We got out safely and before the police came. It would have been a bit difficult explaining, or for them to believe, that we were witnessing to people.

Chapter 5 – God's Guidance

Being in that team taught me a lot for the future, and one Saturday I went with them to a one-day training course in Reading with George Verwer. Operation Mobilization was just beginning. It was probably around 1963. We had an encouraging talk from George and were sent out in twos with a packet of leaflets. They allocated a road to us where we were supposed to knock on every door and speak to people about the Lord. Unfortunately, neither I, nor the girl I was with, had the courage to do this sort of witnessing. So we just pushed the leaflets under each door and of course we were the first ones back in the hall. George Verwer was on his knees fervently praying for us all hoping that Reading would be won for the Lord. He looked up when we arrived because we were the first ones back. He came to ask us how we had got on. To our shame, we had to admit to what we had done. George was very kind and took time to encourage us and told us how to do better in the future.

At this time I was enjoying a relationship with someone from this group and through our friendship came my desire to serve the Lord full time wherever he would send me. There are many people God places in our paths that leave footprints in our lives to bless us and teach us. I know that through this group my life changed positively and prepared me for the future.

Later, I went with this group on a trip to Barcelona. We travelled from London, crossed the English Channel, then through France where we stayed in the Operation Mobilization centre and then went directly to Spain the day after. Once we arrived we divided into smaller groups. I was assigned to a group of missionaries and was to assist them in whatever they needed. It was around 1963 and at this time Protestantism was prohibited in Spain. We had Bibles and Christian literature hidden in our bus and we were very nervous when we arrived at the border. Once there, we had to step out and the bus had to be inspected. We were all very nervous waiting outside the bus praying while they checked it. All the items were in the very back of the bus - halfway through their inspection they received a call and had to leave, but before that they stamped our passports and apologised for making us wait.

When we arrived in Barcelona I went with the American Missionaries who taught me what we were going to do there. We visited families and testified wherever we went. On Sunday we went to church where my friend preached and it was such a special message for me. He spoke about Exodus and Moses. He said that when we use our God-given talents, simple as they might be, God will use them if we offer them to him. When I think about this message now, I know how big an impact it had in my life.

Our friendship began to grow and I really thought that here was the person I would spend my life with. However, during the coming months life took on a different turn and our time together ended. I am very grateful for that friendship. I learnt so much during that time. Maybe most of all was the fact that a person began to come first and the Lord took on second place. When we parted I knew that the Lord had some reason in it all and I began to search for His will for me. A phrase so well-known and not at all biblical ran through my mind, "when God closes a door He always opens a window".

For me, really searching for God's will in my life, I began to hear the word "Missionary". All this time I was very active in the Church. I was a Sunday school teacher and very busy with the Life Boys. I was out evangelising too, and involved in young people's meeting after church on Sundays. I hardly had time to breathe and it was such a fulfilling time, but at the back of my mind I knew that the Lord had something more for me to do. I was listening and waiting for the Lord to speak.

One Sunday Pastor Nash spoke about missions. I know to this day just where I was sitting on that Sunday when God spoke to me though that message. I went home and went to my room and knelt before the Lord and said, "Lord, if you really are speaking to me I have ten reasons why I am not sure I am very suitable material. But if YOU answer these ten questions, then I will go, because I really do need such a firm conviction that this is your will." In a short space of time the Lord spoke to me on all ten questions. I was now convinced that I was hearing the right message from God.

But where I was to go for training? I had no idea. I wrote to various Bible colleges but was turned down by each one because I did not have the right qualifications. I knew that if God had called me HE knew where He was to go to prepare me.

One day, Stan Porter, a missionary from the church, came to see my dad as missionary secretary. He gave me a magazine and on the back page I saw the name of a bible school that I had not written to before. So I sent off my testimony and they accepted me for three years. The bible school was the "Bible College of Wales" in Swansea. The downside was that I had to live in.

I had read many books about missions including one by C T Studd, the founder of WEC International. This book really set me on fire. Here was a man who trusted God completely and told absolutely no-one about his needs. He prayed, and it seemed to me, that instantly God answered him very quickly and easily. So I decided that as I was going to a Bible school where they also trusted God for all their needs, I would start right then and there and so I gave away all my savings. According to C T

Studd, I thought the Lord would miraculously supply my fare for Bible College right then – but nothing came.

It was getting horribly near to the time I was to leave to catch my train and nothing had come for the fare. I really thought I had made a terrible mistake. I was crazy to give away all my savings. I should have at least kept the fare to get me to Bible school. Then my Mother called me and said that the old lady next door wanted to say goodbye to me. "Say goodbye to me?" At this moment I wasn't going anywhere without money. I went to say goodbye and the dear lady gave me an envelope and said she was sorry, she wanted to buy me something but had not been able to get to the shops. Inside was my train fare! So maybe this did work after all. I was to experience many trials in the learning process about trusting God for all my needs. I also learnt that C T Studd had not found it so easy either. I was on my way to Bible College.

So my training began. I was not too sure what to expect and, in some ways, I thought it was going to be easy. After all, I came from a Christian family, had spent all my life in the church, I ran a successful Boys Brigade group, and had spent a lot of time already serving the Lord. But what I did not reckon on was having to share a room with six other women. I was used to having my own room and lots of space for my belongings, but here I was with a night table and only one family photograph allowed on top. I also had a very small space behind a curtain for my clothes and, on top of that, had to share a bathroom with all these people. Lord, what are you doing to me?

Then came meal times. Here began a forced diet, because the portions were very small and very tasteless. During the first weeks we were privileged to receive an abundance of broad beans from a local farmer. I was not aware that you could make so many different meals with broad beans, but even trying to disguise them in many different ways, they were never my favourite vegetable.

To add to my misery we had to get up at the crack of dawn and make our way to the pantry where we were given the job of preparing the vegetables for lunchtime. A huge sack of potatoes or carrots was placed in front of us to peel. After this duty we went to have breakfast and then wash up, followed by prayer time. After prayers it was time to go to the classroom for the lectures. The days took on a routine - lunch, wash-up, and more lessons. We also had to do housework, lots of reading and I had to find time to do my washing, write letters, lots of prayer times and evening talks from the staff.

I found some things very difficult to accept. The college rules were made clear to us in the first days of arriving. One of the rules I really protested about. It was taken very seriously if you were seen talking to or looking at the men students. As you walked to and from lectures you were not allowed to greet or even look at a male student. Now look at things from my point of view, this place was the ideal hunting ground for me to find my future husband. Where better than at Bible Missionary School to find the Prince Charming who had, up until now, slipped past me! To be told that it was forbidden to make friendships was crazy. So one day I asked for an interview with my tutor. However, when I sat before her I found it very hard to put my complaint into words. She gave me the answer (which I have forgotten now) but I realised that rules had been made because of experience and not in order to make life harder.

There was another time when I asked for an interview. I was now in my second year and this time I had to share a room with a girl who was completely the opposite to me. I liked the window open for fresh air, she liked it shut. I was the most orderly person you can find, she was totally disorganised and her half of the room looked like a rubbish dump. My half was spotless and not one thing out of place. Now this became too much for me so at my interview I asked to be transferred to another room. "No, Janet. That is precisely the reason why you have been placed with Juliet. We noticed during last term that you did not get on with her and you need to learn a lesson here. Maybe when you get to the mission field you will have someone like Juliet who you cannot get on with but you have to find a way in order to live with the situation and accept others who are not the same as you." So I had to go back to my room and learn to live with Juliet. We never became the best of friends but I learnt a lesson and found a way to look for the good things in her and appreciate them.

Before I went to Bible school I had never heard that one could trust the Lord for everything, but here, in this place, all of the staff and students were in the same situation. At first it was like an adventure but as time went by, and there was so much to learn in this walk of faith, it seemed to get harder to trust the Lord to supply all one's needs. There was also a rule that you were not to leave for the holidays until you had paid all your fees for that term. Another difficulty was that as the students went home one by one, the workload was harder because those who were left had to do the jobs of the others.

On one of these times of testing I had the money to pay my fees but not for my train fare. I was waiting for the Lord to open up the heavens for me and miraculously send me the money so that I could go home for a while. I remembered that a student once gave a testimony of how he went to the train station and stood in line and the man in front of him gave him the money for his ticket. Well, I would do the same then. If it worked for him it could work for me. So with a lot of faith and a few doubts I set off walking to the station, because I did not have the money for the bus. I arrived at the station and chose the longest line of people buying tickets. I thought the long line would give the Lord time to nudge someone about my need. The line grew shorter and shorter and not one single person seemed to even notice me. The way back to Bible school seemed much longer that the way into town, and the welcome I received was kind too. Thankfully no-one laughed.

My time in Wales was so good for me and I learnt very special lessons for the future. In Colombia I have often needed to trust the Lord for many things and He did not fail me. Prayer was another area that I needed to learn a lot about and I was privileged to be in Bible School during the six-day war in Israel.

When the radio announced the war, the Director, Rev. Howels, called us all to prayer. Classes stopped and only the most necessary duties were carried out. We had one meal a day and all the rest of the time we were on our knees praying. I have never before or since spent so much time on my knees in prayer. But an amazing thing happened. On the 5th day, as we prayed, one of the staff began to pray saying "Thank you, Lord, it is all over!" Through the room there went what was like a gentle breeze and we all began to stand up and praise the Lord that the war was at an end. The Director had been praying in his room but he too had sensed the same as we had, the war was over. That afternoon studies and duties were resumed and the next day the news came through, yes the war had ended. It was apparently the shortest war ever. I really felt it was so special to have been in that room and sensed the Lord's presence there.

In the third year I was placed to help in a Methodist church in Swansea. I met the Mostyn family and for years corresponded with them. We got on so well. They always gave me a good meal too! It was good to be out and serving the Lord. My duties were the women's meeting and visiting those who were lonely or sick. Then one day the Pastor told me that as the University was beginning term I was to go to the meeting for Christians. Well, they turned out to be far from Christian and put me through some very difficult times with their questions, trying to trip me up.

One day, after the meeting, I went back to college with tears in my eyes because they really had made a fool of me. I went to my tutor and said I really found so difficult to go to those meetings. I was given good advice for the following week. Walk into the room head held high, make them sit down, speak with authority and give your testimony. That should make them think. That is just what I did. Never again did they make fun of me and several accepted the Lord as their Saviour.

My time in Swansea was coming to an end and I was praying about my future. Where did the Lord have a place for me? I prayed and searched the library for guidance and strangely enough it came through a book I found about Colombia, but it was about the time of violence and the pictures were awful, scenes of torture and suffering. However, the idea came to me that this was a nation which needed Jesus Christ as saviour. The idea grew and I became convinced that this was God's calling. I was in contact with WEC International and in an interview they advised me to go to London and take a course in medicine for missionaries. I did this and with a friend from bible school, Laurane and I set out for the big city.

Chapter 6 – Steps to a New Future

The Missionary School of Medicine was held near Great Ormond Street hospital in London. From the first day I really found the course so interesting. We were a small group with some students from Europe and a few from England. The time was spent both in studies in class and in the doctors' consultation rooms. We also attended operations. In between classes we went to local hospitals and to the casualty units where we saw some gory sights. We had Christian doctors who came to give us classes on various subjects. One doctor taught us about eye diseases and he invited us all to his home in Kent for a BBQ.

He showed me a lot of interest and invited me to stay a bit longer and said he would take me home later. Well, we got talking with his parents by the fireside and then they invited me to stay the night. Next day a red sports car was waiting for me at the front gate. Wow! I was bowled over. Later that same week he invited me out for a meal, then to a concert and so it began, and I was in a whirl emotionally. One day I told my friend about all this. She worked as a secretary for a doctor and she asked him if he knew this doctor. Joy phoned me straight away. "Janet, be very careful, he is a Don Juan, takes girls out and drops them all the time." But of course I was sure I was different!

Then my friends John and Mary Buck heard about it and invited me over one weekend to talk to me. They were very frank. I needed to get my emotions in order. I was so desperate to get married I was even willing to give up all that the Lord had taken me through. They pleaded with me to give the Lord the most precious desire and allow Him to be my guide. They went upstairs and left me to spend time thinking and praying. It was a real battle. I knew that the Lord was speaking to me but I was not willing to give in. It then came to mind about Abraham who was willing to give his most precious son to God. I too would give the Lord my will and emotions and He would undertake for me.

I lay down on the carpet and gave myself to the Lord, from my fingertips to my toes. "Lord, I am yours - take me and use me for your glory. I slept well that night and so did John and Mary after such a long prayer session praying for me. Back in Medical School for Missionaries the doctor had finished his classes and I never saw him again. But I was first in the eye exam!

Now it was Christmas time and after Christmas my friend Joy Taylor (Sampson) invited me to go and live with her and two other girls in her flat. What super times we had together. They helped me a lot with my studies too. I now began seriously to ask the Lord to guide me as to which mission I should apply for candidate training. I had been in contact with WEC International since bible school so one weekend, when they invited me to go out to Bulstrode (the WEC HQ) I went to talk with the candidate leaders, and it was arranged that I attend the autumn 3 months candidates' course in September.

The Missionary School of Medicine closed classes in June but before we finished we had exams. The last test on a Friday evening before a week of rest was a practical first aid exam. The principal put us into pairs for this exam. I was placed with the Swiss fellow who was very shy. We had to wait ages until we could go into the exam room. About half an hour later we came out of the hospital and began walking home. This Swiss man invited me out for a Chinese meal. I really had my eyes opened because this man was very interesting. When the meal was over we walked all the way home to my flat and then he invited me out the next day, and we spent all week together. At the end of the week he asked me what I was going to do in the holidays. I told him I was going to help out at WEC HQ. "Why there?" he asked. "Because I am going on the candidates' course in September." He asked to which country I had been called. "Colombia," I said. To both of us the surprise came that he too was going on the WEC course in September and then on to Colombia. I still firmly believe that the Lord brought us together.

During the course in Bulstrode we got to know each other better, but we were not allowed to be on our own. Even so the staff were so good to us and we made so many friends. Time grew near when Samuel had to go to Switzerland to finish the course there, but one day Leslie Brierly invited us to tea in his apartment with his wife. To our surprise he told us that he thought we should go to Brazil to open a sending base. Wow! That was going to be difficult. What do we do now? Samuel was due to go to Switzerland in a week. We consulted our leaders, Len and Iris Moules, and they suggested that Samuel should continue with his plans and let the Lord guide us separately. Then if we went to the same country we would have a confirmation of God's calling but if one went to Brazil and the other to Colombia that too would be an answer. It was a very sad parting when Samuel left for Switzerland. We had no idea if we would ever see each other again.

Christmas came and I decided to stay at WEC HQ in order to pray and seek God's will. The same verses constantly came in my daily reading or in the prayer time. It seemed to me that the Lord was doing His utmost to show me His will. The day came when I had to go before the committee to be accepted into WEC. They asked me several questions and then someone said, "What if Samuel is going to Brazil?" "Well", I said, "all I know is that I am going to Colombia."

I was accepted into WEC in January 1970. Then one day after Christmas, while I was helping out at HQ, an announcement came over the tannoy system. "Will Janet please come to reception – there are five letters for her from Switzerland." When I arrived there all the folk from HQ were also there waiting for me to open the letters to find out what Samuel had decided. I went to a place on my own and began with the first one then to the last one. All confirmed that he too was now accepted into WEC for Colombia. I went back to reception and told everyone the news. "Hallelujah!" the crowd shouted. I was so happy!

Neil Row and his wife Mary, who were leaders in the WEC HQ in England, allowed me to phone Samuel in Switzerland and told me that I could go to Switzerland to meet his family, his prayer partners and the Swiss WEC International. I went to Switzerland by train on 19th February, 1970 and Samuel was waiting for me in Zurich. He took me for breakfast and I was so happy to see him again and to be in this beautiful country. It was like a dream come true. I was very much in love and totally sure of being in God's will, knowing I was with the man who was going to be my husband and with whom I was going to serve the Lord.

My parents had already met Samuel and now it was my turn to meet his family. Meeting Samuel's father was what I dreaded because he was not at all pleased that Samuel had an English girlfriend. We arrived earlier than planned and Samuel's father was just coming out of the stable with a wheelbarrow loaded with cow dung, not exactly how he wanted his first impression to be. After lunch I was taken to the lounge to meet his parents officially. His mother was very kind but his father was obviously very wary.

To my surprise, Samuel told me he was leaving at 4pm. A small detail which he had forgotten to tell me was that he still had to do some more training at the Swiss HQ for about two months. So I was left with the family and through sign language we somehow communicated because at the time I did not have any knowledge of the Swiss language and nobody in the family spoke English.

Samuel's Parents were houseparent's at a children's home called "Gott Hilft", which means "God's Help". Well, I truly needed God's help those first few days! I made it clear that I wanted to help in whatever way I could but, oh dear, what a surprise on that first Monday morning. To understand the following, I will tell you that my father always cleaned our shoes back at home. In England this was a man's job. Well dressed in an apron loaned by Samuel's mother, and following behind her, I understood she was taking me to my first job. She opened a door into a very large room where many people changed their shoes before going into the house in slippers. That room was full of boots, Sunday shoes, work shoes, climbing boots; you name it, in that room there was every kind of shoe for every kind of occasion. To my horror my job until lunch time was to clean all those shoes. Not only clean them but clean them Swiss style. They had to look like new when I had finished. Mother-in-law showed me how and then left. She came back 3 hours later to collect me and take me to lunch. I continued my job until tea time at 4pm then a little more until meal time at 6pm. I really wondered what I had let myself in for and if my dad could have seen me he would have laughed very much. But, I thought, if this is a trial made for me by his dad to see if this English girl was any good then I would show them what I was made of. I did my very best with that shoe-cleaning job.

My room was at the top of the house and what a view I had. I was so happy in that little attic room. It was like I was dreaming – some days I could hardly believe what was happening to me. I was slowly learning to communicate in Swiss but the one difficulty was my future father-in-law. That man put me through all sorts of tests trying to prove that the English are lazy. He took me up mountains and down dales, all in one Sunday afternoon. He gave me so much hard work to do and he watched me all the time. One day he came into the kitchen to see what I was up to. The boys and I were clearing up the kitchen after lunch. It was unknown to me but these boys were playing tricks on me and teaching me the wrong names for things. They said a knife was a table, a fork was an aunty and so on. They said and I repeated, and I tried to remember all this. Well my future father–in-law heard the boys and was very angry with them. I was released from kitchen duty and the boys got extra work to do.

I was at the home two weeks and Samuel came at weekends to see me but sometimes he had to go out preaching too. I was told that his parents were going on holiday and, not knowing what to do with me, they took me with them. What a treat, way up in the mountains in a hotel. One day I met a dear old lady who was also staying there and she spoke perfect English. She heard how difficult it was for me to communicate with Samuel's parents and she offered to invite us all to tea one afternoon and interpret for me so that I could express my gratitude to them and give them my testimony.

This was so helpful and at last Samuel's father accepted me, and from then on he started to teach me Swiss and at last he gave his approval to my friendship and future courtship with his son. On 5th April 1970 we became engaged in Zizers Graubunden, Switzerland. It is the custom in Switzerland to buy the wedding ring for the engagement – well that was what we did anyway. The ring is put on the right hand for the engagement and changed over at marriage. I had Samuel's ring engraved inside and very romantically put the verses from scripture, Ruth chapter 1 verse 16 - "Entreat me not to leave you for where you go I will go and where you lodge I will lodge; your people shall be my people and your God my God." To my surprise, Samuel put the whole of Proverbs 31 - the virtuous woman! What a lot to live up to!

One of the things Samuel had to do while we were in Switzerland, making arrangements for our wedding, was to pack up his room in the

"Gott-Hilft" home because when we returned we would be loaned an apartment. Sorting out a cupboard, he came across a new black suit which he knew was not his. It was such very good quality and, not knowing who had left this suit in his cupboard, he took it to his Mother for her to find the owner. A few days later she told Samuel that no one had claimed it. She suggested that he tried it on to see if it fitted him and it did, perfectly. He did not have a suit for the wedding so she let him keep it. Examples like this were what we experienced many times during those days of preparation for our wedding and for the future. We were to be married in Switzerland at the registry office but for us the marriage began after the church service in England. We were actually married twice!   My parents took charge of the organisation and arranged everything for us.

However, when we arrived in England, a month before the wedding, I still did not have a wedding dress. One day, my friend Joy Sampson (later Taylor) told me she had saved up some money so that I could go with her to buy my dress. What a dream! Bit by bit as the days went by the Lord supplied all our needs. Friends came with gifts and often with just what we needed. But a couple of days before the big day I still had no shoes to wear. I was in the garden one day painting an old pair white when a friend came and, to my surprise, my Mum sent her through to me and of course she saw what I was doing. Horrified, she told me to get ready because she was taking me shopping. She bought me not just one pair of shoes but two! I was so happy.

So on 11th July at 11.00am, all dressed in white, I was taken to the church with my Dad and driven there in John Buck's new white car. I arrived in time and the church was packed. So many people came to wish us well and to join us in the ceremony and to bless us. What a happy day that was for me. My parents had arranged for the wedding meal to be held in the church hall adjoining the church. Later we showed slides of Samuel's family and where he lived. His parents were not able to come to the wedding, but they were represented by Samuel's friends, Mr and Mrs Gausen. They were house parents to children from missionaries working with the OMF - Samuel had lived with them before going to Missionary School of Medicine to learn English. Later we went home to my parents' to change and go to London and then we went onto Switzerland for our honeymoon.

Our honeymoon was rather different to what I imagined. Samuel told me that his uncle had loaned us a holiday chalet way up in the mountains above Chur in Graubunden. You maybe have seen those photos in Swiss calendars - those little dream places up on the slopes among the cows with bells, and the little stream running by. Well it was something like that but a little path went along outside our window. It was the short cut to the local farm where it seemed that half the population went daily to buy milk!

Then Samuel's youngest brother wanted to try out his new tent. Apart from that his uncle felt it necessary to join us almost daily to see how we were getting on. One day we were up very early and Samuel and I went on a wonderful long walk right up in the mountains. We came home early that day, rather tired after so much walking. Inside our dream place we had to undress downstairs because we slept up in the roof, it was so small. Along came Samuel's uncle for his usual visit - what an embarrassing moment, because Samuel had to ask him to hand us our clothes so that we could come down. Our accompanied honeymoon came to its close and it was time for us to start the next phase of our preparations. We visited some prayer groups and we prepared for our time in Spain for language study.

Samuel bought two VW cars – one had been in an accident and was damaged at the front and the other at the back, and to my utter amazement he made a perfect car out of those two wrecks. What a genius - I was very impressed with this husband of mine.

So in August we set out for Spain, driving through France and into Spain to Madrid. We had our tent and so camped on the way. About three days after we arrived we went to the home of a contact we were given by the WEC. A dear couple found us accommodation, which was very hard to find in Madrid and more so because of our limited income. The apartment was very small to say the least. In the only bedroom there was room for just one single bed. Samuel had to sleep on a camp bed in the dining room, which was also small, but in the centre was a huge round table with a huge chandelier hanging from the middle of the ceiling.

The kitchen, along with the rest of the place, was so small it had space for one person at a time to use it. Now the bathroom was a joke - you could be on the toilet, wash your hands and shower at the same time, remembering first of all to take the ladder down from the wall and the ironing board and broom out!

We started language studies in Madrid but it soon became obvious that this system of studying was not working for me. I had been learning Swiss and German up until a week before we left for Spain and my mind could only bring back those two languages at that time. It was too soon after learning the other two to begin a third one. So, to my great disappointment I had to drop out. However, at the same time I found out that I was expecting our first child. We were so happy and daily put into practice what we had learnt at the medical course. I did not go to a doctor once in Spain because we were advised that sometimes one came away with more illness than one went with and, as we had no insurance, that was what we had to do.

I was very frustrated and lonely - my husband was away all morning and with such a small place the cleaning was done in 10 minutes. The sun only entered the apartment 20 minutes each day and I was also very scared to go out because I had no way of communicating with anyone. Then one day a neighbour across the way came when Samuel was home and invited us to go to visit them in the evening to watch the news on TV. This was so good for us. It meant I could get out a bit and Samuel could practice his Spanish, which he was learning very quickly. I think this family took us in as a challenge. The lady took me shopping, visiting or whatever each day to teach me Spanish and this was perfect for me. We became very good friends and for many years after we communicated with them.

At this time the WEC opened Spain as a new field and Irene and Wesley Driver arrived in Madrid to start the work there. They were like angels sent to us to help us. As I grew bigger with the pregnancy it was impossible to get under the shower in our tiny bathroom and so we went once a week for a long dip in Wesley and Irene's wonderful bathtub. She always had something wonderful ready to eat, and it was super to speak in my own language. Although Samuel and I always conversed in English, this was different and it was women's talk - about babies mostly.

In the building we were living in there was a place on the ground floor that sold churros and chocolate every morning. This enticing aroma seemed to invite us to have breakfast the same way as the Spaniards do. However, money was scarce and we looked for ways to eat as cheaply as possible. One day Samuel came home with an armful of milk bottles. There was a special offer at a local market for pasteurised milk. Buy one get one free. Samuel, forever the bargain hunter, could not resist this. Soon our tiny abode began to fill up with milk bottles - all round the walls was a line of bottles. Each time he bought milk he was given a receipt. But when it came time to return the empty bottles Samuel found that he had lost the receipts. This was no problem, the man at the local market said he should not worry he would never forget Samuel because he had never sold so much milk to anyone before!

We were in Spain for about six months but we looked forward to going back to Switzerland. Sometimes on a Sunday afternoon we would walk to the bridge that went over the road leading out of Madrid to the motorway, and then we walked back to the flat. In our calculations our baby would arrive around the 11th April and so we left Madrid about three weeks before that date. It was the end of March and, for various reasons, there would be no camping this time, so we stayed in hotels along the way. Our little car was loaded to the brim with our belongings with a first-aid kit near at hand in case Samuel had to deliver our baby on the way. Driving through Spain and coming into France with this huge bundle in front of me was rather uncomfortable but we stopped when necessary for a walk and to eat. In France we drove on and on but when it was late and it had begun to snow we started looking for somewhere to stay. We were now up in the mountains and at last we found a little inn. The owner and his wife welcomed us in to a lovely lounge with a huge fire in the fireplace. The couple were so kind to us and I believe they were wondering if they were receiving Mary and Joseph!

The lady came to our room with a big bowl of hot water for my feet, which were a bit swollen. And then she came with a tray of soup and huge chunks of fresh bread. Oh it was such a feast, and I was so tired. Next day, we set off early in order to be in Switzerland for breakfast. Passing through immigration and into Switzerland we found the first restaurant, which was "Migros", and we had hot coffee and "Burli" bread rolls with fresh jam and butter. We were nearly home. When we arrived in Zizers the family came to greet us and welcome us back.

Now it was time to prepare for our child. I went to the doctor for the first time, two weeks before the baby was due. Both of us were in perfect health. We were loaned an apartment where Samuel's parents lived, and began to get ready for the birth.

I had no idea what was happening the night the contractions began. For all I had read and seen, nothing prepared me for what was in store. Samuel went about midnight to tell his parents about my pains and we were told to go straight to the clinic. It was snowing and very dark. There were road works and the usual route to the hospital was closed. I was starting to feel panic, but eventually we arrived. All night I laboured and in the morning, at 8am on 21st April, with the birds singing outside the window, our son was born. He was so big - he weighed 10 pounds - but he was perfectly healthy. Later, in September, when we were on our way to Colombia I realised what a blessing it was that he was a big healthy baby.

I was in the hospital for ten days, which was normal in those days. It was like being in a hotel. The only problem was that I longed to get home and start to look after my son, because he was in the nursery all the time except when it was feeding time. At last it was time to go home and Samuel collected me and drove at a snail's pace because he was so nervous about having the baby in the car. When we arrived home everyone was so happy with baby Sami and we were the proud parents too.

Chapter 7 - Colombia

At this point, I look back to so many wonderful examples of God's guidance and provision. I am amazed at how the Lord Himself gave me so much ability to do the Bible College training, the Medical Course for Missionaries, and learn two more languages - Swiss and German. It seems like I learnt more in the last ten years than in all my youth.

Life held so many wonderful possibilities and we set out for Colombia with such a passion to serve the Lord, quite literally not knowing what Colombia was really like. We visited several prayer groups in Switzerland and then when our son Sami was three months old we went to England to say goodbye to my family and friends there. We had a farewell service in our church at Leigh Road when the Pastor and deacons prayed for us and commissioned us to serve the Lord.

Then once more we went back to Switzerland for the final packing. Everything was going as planned when we had news from Colombia that we should not apply for a visa, as the President of Colombia, Ismael Botero, was not allowing evangelicals to enter the country as missionaries.

This news was quite amazing. "What now?" we asked. We were ready to go, baggage packed, and now this. How strange are God's ways sometimes. We were praying with many friends about this situation when one day friends of WEC Switzerland HQ phoned Samuel to say that there was an advertisement in the local paper saying that the Colombian government were looking for professionals in certain jobs to go to Colombia as immigrants. In that list was the word "Agriculturalists" - which stood out so clearly to us.

So, loaded with all of Samuel's diplomas and certificates, we headed for Bern to the offices of the Colombian Embassy. Everything began to happen very quickly and we were accepted. Samuel said that we wanted to work with the evangelical church and we were told, "What you do in your spare time is your concern".

We were given guidelines about the contract with the government - we had two years to organise and set up a working farm. We would be going by boat and two thirds of the trip was paid for by the government. We could take a huge amount of luggage but we had very few things. It all was amazing. That is how the Lord opened up the way for us to go to Colombia. During the following years we were very aware that it was such a good idea to enter the country under those conditions.

So, Samuel, Janet and Samuel Jr. (with all of 5 months behind him!) were on their way at last! We went from Lanquart station by train to Genoa in Italy - Samuel's father came with us as far as possible. On the 13th September 1971 we arrived at the boat. What emotions we had. We now said the last goodbyes to my father-in-law and climbed up the gangplank and to our separate cabins. Yes, Samuel had to go in with the monks and me with some nuns. Then once we were installed we met on deck to wave goodbye to Samuel's father.

As his father got smaller and smaller and the distance between us got longer and longer the reality began to set in, now there was no turning back, but actually that thought did not enter our heads. No, our adventure was about to begin. What was awaiting us? To be honest, it was like going to the moon without any idea what it would be like. It had been so difficult to get information about Colombia at that time. Hot, yes, it must be hot because it is on the Equator, but then Bogotá is 2,600 meters above sea level, which brings the temperature down somewhat. But first we had to get used to being on board the ship. That in itself was quite an adventure. I was in a cabin with my little son and accompanied by three nuns. My understanding of that sisterhood was very limited, but in those three weeks my eyes were opened to some very different ideas. We had one sink for our ablutions and, my goodness, those women took up so much of the time in front of the mirror - I had no idea they were allowed skin creams and potions! One of those nuns made friends with the man who looked after the cabins and to my amazement invited him in one day. Samuel was learning that the life of a monk was also far from his imagination too.

The ship was Italian so we ate more pasta on that trip than I have ever had in my life, or so it seemed. I had to wash my baby's nappies and hang them out on deck to dry with some lovely Swiss clothes pegs. So when I went to get them later, to my surprise there were no nappies and no clothes pegs either. In future I took a book and sat watching those nappies till they dried.

On that trip we made friends with a very nice man who was a monk. Samuel and I, with Sami asleep in his pram beside us, used to meet up on deck each night before bedtime and we got talking to this man who was very interesting. One day we heard that a monk had died while on the journey and that night our friend did not appear. We never saw him again until one night, to our uttermost horror, coming up the stairs to greet us was "our" monk! We thought we were seeing a vision but, no, there he was in flesh and blood. We told him we were very pleased to see him as we were convinced he had died. He then laughed, and told us that when a Catholic dies, for the next nine nights and days, special prayers are said for him as his soul travels to the next place of rest. That is where the monk had been, guiding his fellow monk to his place of rest. We certainly had a lot to learn about the Catholic faith.

Our ship stopped at one or two places on the way before we set out to cross the Atlantic. This was interesting and it was also good to walk on solid land for a while. Also we got used to seeing different cultures on the way - it was all good preparation for arriving in Colombia.

At last one morning we were up very early because we knew that on this day we would catch our first glimpse of the land where we had chosen to serve the Lord. What an amazing emotion that was for us. We came into the docks - not the best impression, I believe, in any land - but what hit us most was the heat and the shouting in Spanish. They spoke so dreadfully quickly, language school was very different to this! Also, on the coast of Colombia in Cartagena, where we landed, they have a very strong dialect and words sound very different to inland. But we managed.

Our green barrels, containing our belongings, were put on land and we went to the great halls for inspection and permission to enter the country. Two officials took a great likening to our radio, which Samuel had worked so hard to earn enough to buy it. It was so strange to hear this lively music coming out of our radio from which we had heard mostly classical music up till then! We prayed very fervently so that they would let us keep our radio. Then one minute they were called away but they first put stamps on our luggage and the radio, and we were OK. But that was only for a while. We were met outside by Colombian government officials and taken to a hotel for the night and then on to Bogotá next day by plane.

During the night it was very hot and even with air conditioning it was not easy to sleep. Then we heard what I thought were fireworks, never having heard gun shots before, but Samuel had been in the army and he knew what the sounds were. The owner of the hotel came running in with a gun in her hand - my goodness, I thought, this is like the Wild West! Whatever had we got ourselves into? She told us that a few men, who had delivered our luggage that day when we arrived, had come back at night to help us make the journey lighter by taking some of our precious baggage! But she had heard them and they had left, running. She placed a small bed beside our barrels and a young boy slept the rest of the night beside our things. This was our welcome to Colombia!

After a very unusual night without getting much sleep, we went down to the beach to let Sami put his feet in the sea in Cartagena. We then went to the airport, Samuel in a lorry with our barrels and I with Sami and our cases in a taxi. To my amazement, I had to put my feet either side of a hole in the floor. The driver noticed my amazement and said "That, madam, is the air conditioning!" Those people who live on the coast sure are happy souls!

We went by plane to Bogotá. There, the government officials met us again and gave certain instructions. The missionary team were also there to receive us. We stayed with Martha and Ralph Hines, who were our senior missionaries and who became our "parents". They were so kind to us and we spent two months with them in the Barios Unidos church in Bogotá. This was a time for adapting and getting to know something about the culture and some very different ways of doing things. We were taught how to bargain and never pay the asking price. To this day I find this very difficult, although that custom has changed with the big supermarkets in Bogotá with fixed prices, but when we arrived in 1971 so many things had to be learnt.

By the end of November the Colombian Pastors met to decide where we would be placed. We had been preparing for six years and both of us thought we would go to the Indian tribes. Our luggage was like a jungle pack and we had very few clothes for cold Bogotá. So while Ralph was at the meeting with the Pastors, Samuel and I were praying for guidance as to which tribe we would be working in. Ralph came home late but we had to know how the meeting had gone. Well, to our surprise, we were allocated to go to a town not an hour outside Bogotá. It was explained that the Pastors thought it would be good for us to master the Spanish and the culture before going amongst the Indians. After a two-year period our situation would be reconsidered, but we actually never got to even see an Indian tribe.

The next Sunday Samuel went with Ralph to visit Zipaquirá, which was to be our mission field. Samuel came back very enthused and told me what his first impressions were. Soon after, we were on our way again with our few belongings to install ourselves in this famous town - it has an amazing salt mine, the highest in the world above sea level. We arrived in Zipaquirá at the beginning of December and we lived in the church premises which were in the area called "La Floresta".

One night we heard fireworks and there was the dreadful smell of burning tires. We ventured out to see what was going on. It seemed very strange to us that in the middle of the street there was this bonfire with a tyre on top. The people were in a very festive mood too. Samuel asked our neighbour what was going on. It was the celebration of the Holy Conception of Maria. Strange, we thought, so near to Christmas too. Surely it should be nine months before, but we soon learnt that there were many practices here in the church which are not in the Bible but are fervently carried out and believed in.

So we began our time in that town. Samuel bought some wood and with help made us our beds as we had slept on the floor up until then. We put a plank of wood on top of two barrels and that served as our table. It was all somewhat primitive but we were happy. The missionaries had given us a washing machine, which was already an antique, but served us for a time. We had bought a second hand bed for Sami in Bogotá and a wooden high chair for him too. We lived there for about nine months but because the house was so humid and our books, mattresses and other articles were getting damaged, the mission gave us permission to move, and Samuel soon found us a house not far away – this was bigger and had a terrace.

One Tuesday Samuel arrived back from the open market with some vegetables, some fruit and a little black dog under his arm! Nero was our first pet.   We were one step towards our farm, which the government had given us two years to establish. Next came some chicks which Samuel had in a pen. Sami was delighted with all these new toys, especially Nero, who became a firm friend and he sometimes shared the playpen with Sami.

Chapter 8 – Early Days in Colombia

One day a dear old lady, who was one of the few believers who attended our meetings, came to ask Samuel, "Pastor, what programme is planned for Christmas?" We looked at each other – Christmas, surely it was not Christmas time! We had bright, sunny, hot days, no snow, no cold winds, nothing to remind us that it was Christmas time. But yes, it was the 20th December and it did seem so weird to us with this weather. We were both used to Christmas being different, but now we were in another land and we had to move with time and customs very different to what we were used to. For a start, not one Christmas card came. No-one had sent anything, or so we thought, but of course packages took up to six weeks to arrive at that time. Around about February we received some cards!

Christmas day came and I felt so sad - it was all so different for us. Then that same dear old lady came to visit us. Abigail brought us two presents. There was one present for me - a pair of stockings, but she was very short and they only came up to my knees! And a cake which maybe had a long history, because it was so dry - it was like eating a biscuit but, no matter, as we say, it was the thought that counts. Samuel went to the market and came home with a pineapple, which I was used to seeing come out of a tin. This pineapple had a very different, fresh taste and we really enjoyed it.

Our first year in Colombia went by very quickly. We were often enthused but sometimes things were not so easy. The attendance at our meetings varied in numbers constantly and only a handful of them really followed the Lord. Sometimes the little meeting room was full and then sometimes just eight or ten people came. However, this was a very special time for Samuel, and I was so proud of him, he had so many amazing ideas for church growth. The Christians were so new to believing in God's word and following Him, but it was difficult sometimes. Those that were with us then are still here in Colombia and still faithful believers. I remember Martha Florez and her sons, Edgar, Orlando and Arturo; Gloria Baracaldo, her children, Janet, Omar, Javier, Mike and the youngest, Yvonne; Alcira Ramirez, with her children, Claudia, Sandra, Herman, and Ricardo. Martha and Edgar were the first two that Samuel baptised.

Samuel was asked to visit some churches and family groups along a river called "the Black River" and it was just that - when it rained hard the water was black like coal. He went once a month, just taking his Bible, a toothbrush and a change of clothes. He had to travel by bus for about five hours and those journeys were very difficult for him as he was travel sick. It was also not very safe. This area was dangerous and, being a foreigner, he was exposed to the rebels, but the Lord kept him safe. Later, the journey became easier for him when he bought a very old Land Rover.

I was on my own while he visited these groups. I did not find it very easy being left alone, with no means of communicating with him and with a young son growing quickly. I had so little experience as a mother, and I remember I went everywhere with my Dr Spock baby book!

We had been in Zipaquirá 18 months when we had to give a report to the national church about our work during that time. We felt very frustrated because really there was so little growth, and at the end it was decided to close the place where we met and to continue in our home.

For me, the first year was a huge mixture of learning. I was learning Spanish from Samuel and also a dear lady from the church, Martha Florez, took me under her wing and became my very special friend and teacher. She taught me Spanish, and how and what to buy at the market, she showed me which were fruit and which were vegetables because there were so many wonderful varieties to choose from. She was so patient with me and I thank the Lord today for Martha, who really is an amazing woman.

We often laughed together at my Spanish or the things I got mixed up with when I bought fruit thinking it was vegetables! One day I bought what I thought was a marrow. So I made soup - it was horrid. Martha turned up so I gave her some. "Janet, whatever is this?" "Soup," I said. She asked to see what I had used, so I showed her. She laughed - it was a papaya!

There was so much to learn and I had a small son to look after too, and no-one to get advice from. The missionaries came from Bogotá to visit us quite often but I still found it difficult. I was always tired too, the altitude affected me and I was often anaemic. Our day began at 6am - the sun rises at the same time every day, and goes down at 6pm every day, all year round. This took some getting used to. No seasons either, but lovely weather all year round. Colombia is a very beautiful country and I enjoyed the countryside when we could get out.

One day we went to visit some ladies from the church who had invited me to have an afternoon meal with them. They sat me in the dining room and departed for the kitchen, which was very close. They then carried on this strange conversation about me, thinking I couldn't understand because I could not speak Spanish very well. "What do you think she would like to eat? Poor thing she can hardly talk. Nice dress she has on." And so it went on. I sat there feeling so stupid. Years later we once more met up for tea. I told them about that time when I could understand but couldn't express myself - we all laughed.

Some days I felt so frustrated because it seemed that I was doing nothing towards winning or even speaking to people about the Lord. Six years preparing to get to Colombia and now what? One day I spoke to my leader, Martha Hines, she was always so wise and encouraging. "Janet," she said, "you make lovely cakes and biscuits. When Samuel has visitors, offer them your cooking and in that way you are serving the Lord." My goodness, I thought, instead of six years preparing in so many different ways, I should just have done a cookery course! Well I did put her advice into practice and I can tell you how the Lord used my biscuits.

One day I noticed my neighbour across the road hanging out her washing on her terrace. I waved to her. We began to greet each other. Then I remembered the advice that Martha Hines had given me, so I took her some biscuits. She liked them and asked me if I would teach her how to make them. Soon after that I invited her to my kitchen and we made biscuits, mostly by sign language, but we became friends.

In 2010 I was preaching in the first church we founded in Zipaquirá and a lady came and spoke to me after the service. "Janet," she said, "do you remember me?" Well, it was nearly 40 years ago since we had lived in Zipaquirá. I told her I was sorry but I could not remember her name. She told me that I taught her mother how to make my biscuits and because of that all her family were now Christians. I remembered that I had taken my goodies to my neighbour to make conversation. Somehow through that meeting, she came to our church and became a Christian and now all of the family were walking in God's ways. So just sharing biscuits can also be a means of evangelising.

In those first months in Zipaquirá so many weird and wonderful things happened to us. We were so new to the culture and we had to learn lots of things through experience. One day Samuel opened the door to a man who told us he was from one of the churches Samuel had visited.

He asked if we could help him buy a coffin for his mother who had died in the nearby hospital. We had very little money but found enough to give him some and he went on his way. About a month later once more Samuel opened the door and there stood a dear lady asking if we had seen her son. Oh dear, yes, we had given him the money to buy her coffin!

On another occasion three little children knocked on the door at lunch time one day to ask if we had any food, so I gave them something to eat. They then kept turning up at lunch time. One day my friend Martha was with me when the children came. She suggested we went with them to get to know their mother and maybe talk to her about the Lord. So next time we went with the children. What a surprise when we came to a nice house and there was the mother waiting with the dinner cooking for the children. She was horrified when she knew they had been calling regularly at my house for a meal. They told her, they liked the foreigner's cooking!

Chapter 9 – Expanding the Family

1972 was a busy year. I was expecting my second child and I was somewhat apprehensive as to where my baby would be born. The local hospital was not the cleanest or most modern place. When I had visited someone there I definitely was not very happy at the prospect of my child being born there, but it seemed there was little choice.

One day, not long before the suggested date of birth, Samuel came home with the news that he had found a private clinic in the town, newly built and just opened. We went to investigate and what a wonderful surprise. It was clean, new and up-to-date in technology (well, for 1972). So we made an appointment to visit the doctor. To our surprise the doctor had been in England and studied at Oxford. He spoke very good English and for me, just learning Spanish, this was ideal. We began to pray and trust that we would be able to pay the bill for this clinic when the time came, and our family in Switzerland sent us a money gift, which covered my stay in hospital. We were so grateful to them.

The doctor said that my baby would probably arrive on my birthday and, if so, he would bring me an English breakfast! Well my birthday came and went and no baby had arrived - so I thought, no English breakfast for me - but on the evening of the 8th of October my pains began.

About midnight, more or less, we went to the clinic. Samuel went to park the car and I entered on my own. Two nice young nurses came to greet me. Now, what I am going to tell you is not so funny in English, but in Spanish there is a separate word for when an animal gives birth compared to when a human gives birth. Remember, I was still learning Spanish, and had only heard terms for birth used for animals. So I proudly announced that I had come to give birth - like the cows! These two dear nurses could not hide their surprise and behind their hands were laughing. Samuel appeared, and wanted to know what I had told them. I proudly told him, and he also laughed, and then rectified my mistake. But the story circulated round the hospital - I was to go down in history as the first woman to give birth using the same name as for giving birth to the cows.

Miriam arrived safe and sound early next morning on Tuesday 9th October. Outside the window it was market day. So she came into to the world to the sound of the sheep and chickens and other animals. The doctor later appeared with an English breakfast, even though it was not my birthday! I enjoyed that meal very much. It was not easy to get bacon, cornflakes and marmalade in Bogotá in those days. When we took Miriam home Sami was overjoyed - here was a playmate for him. He was very impatient and wanted to play NOW. But this little sister was asleep all the time. He would go and wake her up, so we had to put a lock on the door so she could sleep. Sami and Miriam were always together and are still good friends.

In November Samuel's parents came to visit us for the first time. One night we were in bed when we heard sounds outside the house, and a voice calling us. It was the voice of his father. We could hardly believe it, but there, standing outside, was my mother- and father–in–law, accompanied by a taxi and a young man. Quickly we went downstairs to let them in.

A few months earlier we had received a letter telling us the date of their arrival, but they had changed the date. As a letter took six weeks to get to Colombia, we received the news two weeks after they arrived. The story on how they arrived at our doorstep was amazing. Having waited hours at the airport for us to turn up, they went to the offices of Lufthansa airlines asking them to help get them to Zipaquirá. They did not have our address, and we had no telephone. A taxi was arranged and off they went, with not a word of Spanish between them. They arrived in the main square of our town, very late at night. The only person in sight was a young man on his way home. The taxi driver asked if he knew any Swiss people in the town. Yes, he was attending our church, and took my in-laws to our front door! This experience is a testimony to the protection and guidance of our Lord. All sorts of dreadful things could have happened, but they arrived safe and sound, right to our front door.

We had no beds ready for them but quickly organised ours and, after talking about this amazing experience and having something to eat and drink, we once more settled down to sleep. Sami was 5 months old when we said good-bye to his grandparents and so he was amazed next morning, to find two strangers in our bed. Samuel's parents were with us for about three months and they loved Colombia. I was very pleased for the help they gave us, because with two small children and the work in the church, it was not easy. But I was also glad they were there because in December I received the sad news that my dear Dad had died. A missionary came from Bogotá with a telegram from Mum that on 19th December Dad had passed away.

I was devastated. I last saw my Dad waving goodbye as we set off to Switzerland to go to Colombia in the September. I had no thought that it would be the last time I saw him. I wanted to go to England for the funeral but it was impossible. I remember I went to Bogotá on my own, in some vain hope that someone would get me to England. The embassy said no, and the missionaries said it was not possible to get permission to leave the country having just arrived. At that time it took 6 weeks to get government permission to travel. They checked you were in no trouble with the police, the banks, the town, the tax collector, and all that took 6 weeks. No way could I get to England. I was in shock. I wandered around not really aware where I was going and all at once I came to myself again and had no idea where I was, wandering around somewhere in Bogotá.

If you believe in angels, sent to help us, this was such an occasion. I do. Not having any idea how to get back to Zipaquirá, I went into a shop and asked for help. A kind man took me first by bus to the bus station and told the driver to help me because I was not well and, please, to put me off in Zipaquirá. This he did and I arrived home safely.

If you should ask me what is difficult about missionary life I would say that the separation from family and friends is so hard. Not having them there at times like these. My children had no aunts and uncles. We had no family except when someone came to visit, and that was not very often. When we set out for Colombia I looked forward to the day when my Mum and Dad would see my children. Dad never even received a photograph of Miriam. The photos of her arrived in England two weeks after his death. Can you imagine receiving a letter from your father written before he died and arriving three weeks after? It is a strange feeling. But, looking back, we lived through it and could identify with others who had passed through similar experiences. The missionaries and Samuel's parents were so good to me. There is always a positive side to look at.

Samuel's parents visiting us enabled me to accompany Samuel on a trip to coffee country [a hotter area of the country, at a lower altitude than Bogotá] where there were several groups of Christians that Samuel visited each month. I was really glad I could at last go on one of these missionary trips. We left early one day and went by bus on an unpaved road for about four hours or more. We arrived in a town called La Palma, stayed the night with the Pastors, and Samuel spoke at the evening service.

Very early next day we set off, on foot, along the horse trail. There were no maps to follow, just where the horses walked, that was our street guide. It is very hot in this part of Colombia and banana trees, oranges and coffee all grow in this climate. We walked for hours, uphill and down dale. We had forgotten to bring water or food with us. By the afternoon I was so tired and we still had a long way to go.

At this point we came to a large river which we had to cross on a rope bridge. This is a bridge made of planks of wood strung together and it moves with every step you take. It is very scary. We sat down on a log to rest a while and an old lady appeared from a nearby house and offered us something to drink. It was sweet and very refreshing and she gave me three large cups to drink (they were more like large, half-coconut shells). Samuel only drank one.

We continued our journey crossing the river, the bridge seemed to sway a lot but I managed to get to the other side. In the heat of the afternoon I was ready for a rest but we had to carry on so that we arrived before dark. Life seemed very funny all of a sudden, and I kept laughing which helped get us to our destination. The last lap was uphill to the house of the believers. Samuel pushed from behind which made me laugh even more. At last we arrived some time before 6pm - we had been walking for some seven hours.

As there is no telephone in the country no-one knew we were coming so once we arrived the children were sent to the surrounding houses to tell the Christians that Pastor Samuel had arrived for a meeting. We were given a meal and lots to drink and then the meeting started. I could hardly keep my eyes open, but these dear people were so thrilled to have us with them. The meeting went on for hours. Lots of choruses were sung and repeated - all by heart. Then Samuel preached for an hour and a half, and finally around 10pm the preaching ended and we went to bed, at last.

The bed, which was given to us, was the only one in the house. The sheets were made from flour sacks opened up and stitched together. The mattress was made of the same material and filled with straw. It was not exactly soft but with the exhaustion I had, no matter what it was like, I soon fell asleep.

Next day I could hardly lift my head from the pillow, it was aching so much. Samuel went in search of an aspirin. Along came Brother Antonio, very serious with a glass of water and an aspirin. "Sister Janet," he said, "last night you arrived here drunk!" Was it possible that I was drunk? I was horrified - my first trip to the Christians there and I arrived drunk? This dear man asked me if, when we reached the river, we accepted a drink from the old lady. I told him "Oh yes, and it was very refreshing." "Dear sister," he said, "that old lady did that as a trick on you. What you drank was fermented rice water, very intoxicating, that is why you arrived drunk!" Oh dear, what fame. The English missionary was drunk on her first trip to coffee country - I never touched that drink again!

We stayed for about two days and then went back – it was a long journey. We were later told that once a week a bus made the trip back to town. Oh, I was so relieved.

Chapter 10 - Fulfilling Government Regulations

You may remember that we had come to Colombia as immigrants and we had a contract with the Government. They had given us two years to get organised and expected that we had at least begun a farming project. Our plan was to concentrate on the church and to bring people to know Christ and then get the building started. Afterwards we would concentrate on the farming.

We had left it a bit late, and time was running out, so we began searching for a suitable piece of land which was not expensive, in the area of Zipaquirá. We searched and searched and at last, when two brothers offered us some land three times, we went one Saturday to have a look and we both thought it was very suitable. On Sunday, after church, we went again to have another look, on our own this time. We decided that this was where we would like to live. It was an enormous step of faith. We had nowhere near the amount of money that they were asking but we decided to walk the land like it says in Joshua 1 v 3: "Every place that the sole of your foot will tread upon I have given you." The Lord gave us both the assurance that we should go forward.

Later we met the two brothers to sign the legal document and we promised to pay the total amount on the given date for completion. It turned out that it took them two years until they were ready to finalise. In that time the Lord had amazingly blessed us and we nearly had our money ready, but we were still short for the final payment. A small inheritance from my Dad came just 6 weeks before the closing date. It was quite amazing how the Lord supplied in many different ways. On a hillside there were eucalyptus trees growing and it was possible to sell those trees to a company, which came and cut them down and took them away for construction. This was just one way the Lord supplied. Our God is a great God.

When we met the two brothers again we invited them for a meal in our home. Normally these deals are completed over a few drinks, and in conversation they told us they thought we were crazy foreigners to go into such a deal with practically nothing in the bank. Those men were very good friends of ours from that time on and often when Samuel was away travelling one of them would come and check that I was OK.

We began building our house on the farm. Once more Samuel showed the builders step by step what they had to do, but now he had more experience. However, before we moved up to live in our own house, while we were still living in the town, I noticed that the front doorstep was wet most mornings. I thought a dog was doing his business there so I scrubbed and put down disinfectant and any awful smelling liquid I could get but still the doorstep was wet. One day I was talking to my neighbour friend and she told me that the wet patch was not from a dog but an old lady was practicing witchcraft on us, to get rid of us. The whole street knew this was happening and were amazed that nothing had worked. It was God's power protecting us.

At last moving day came and we went to live on the farm. I was now pregnant and expecting my third child. When we moved in, the house was not finished - some windows still had no glass in them. We needed doors and it was possible to see the sky through the spaces in the ceiling in our bedroom. And it was very cold. The toilet was not quite ready so when I needed to use the bathroom I took a long stick with a white piece of material tied on and went to enjoy the countryside while sitting in a ditch. This was not exactly fun, but different! I really did appreciate the day the toilet was connected.

We named our farm, "The Upper Room." It became the meeting place for many. We held conferences in the open air for young people, and received visitors from hot country on their way to Bogotá.

In the evening on July 18th 1974 my labour pains began and not long after it was time to go to the clinic. When we went out to the car it wouldn't start. I had to help push it in order to get it going. This time, when I walked into the hospital, I knew the correct words to explain why I was there – well, really no words were needed! I was very worn out by the time Martha came into the world because I was a long time in labour, and this time there was no English breakfast for me. My little baby girl was a fighter and she had lovely blonde hair. The nurses spent their time walking her around the hospital showing the other mothers my beautiful baby with the golden hair.

However, before Martha was born another person joined our family to live with us for many years. One day, a lady in our church asked us if we could help a young girl who had arrived with her sister and new husband and who were living in one room and sleeping in one bed. Elizabeth came to live with us when she was 11 years old. She became part of the family and stayed till she was about 20. I was so glad for her help and when Martha was born she looked after Miriam quite a lot, although Miriam felt that, at two and a half, she did not need looking after. We helped Elizabeth with her schooling and many years later she married one of our young Pastors.

My mother also came to visit us that year, in 1974. What a tremendous help. I really was so weak from the last pregnancy and with two other small children to look after life was very full. Miriam was intrigued with this little sister and one day paid her a visit. Later I went into the bedroom and there was a marvellous smell. My mother had brought me a small bottle of perfume, a very rare article for me in those days, and Miriam had decided to get it down from on top of a cupboard and fill Martha's bed linen with it. The perfume was quite precious and I did not want to wash the bedding for many days after that. I could fill a book with so many incidents and comings and goings in those ten years.

One day, when we were still living in the town, a lady stood on the doorstep and said she was a Christian from one of the small groups Samuel was in charge of. We had only just arrived so we were not sure if this was true or not and we were inclined to believe everyone in those days. She asked me if I would look after her baby for an hour while she went to the hospital for a Doctor's appointment.

I received this small bundle and took the baby to sleep in Sami's bed. As time went past we realised that the Mother had abandoned her baby. We went to the police next day and they took the child into care.

In time the house was finished and we lived there 10 years. We have many happy memories of times together round the fire and at meal times. The children were free to play outside and in the small forest. There was a stream running through the farm and we often went there to rest and play. We had some lovely walks up to the top of the big hill which was part of the farm too. Life was not all hard work; we took time for ourselves now and then.

We saw God's good hand upon us and He prospered us in what we did. One day we went up that hill to take some photographs of the farm, from above, and what a surprise, the land around the farm was dry and the grass looked dead but our land was a bright beautiful green. While we served the Lord He took care of our land.

We did have some difficult times from the neighbours and one old lady had a fear of us. She had a donkey and it was tied up along a path leading to the farm so that the animal could eat the grass. When she saw or heard us coming she would get that donkey back home as soon as possible. Sometime later she had a problem with the water supply so Samuel told her she could come and take water from us, and later he fixed a pipe to her house. Bit by bit she became less cautious of us and one day Samuel asked why she moved the donkey when she saw us coming. The neighbours had told her that we foreigners eat donkey meat!

Chapter 11 - Extending our territory

Now that the church in Zipaquirá was going ahead we decided to evangelise in some of the surrounding towns. This was no easy task. The Catholic faith was very strong, and we often met with open hostility, so when it became clear that this was not the best time, we moved on to further fields. With my friend Martha we decided to go to a small town way out in the country and we valiantly set off in the only bus going that way once a day. The roads were unpaved and the bus, it seemed, had no springs and the seats had been in use many years. It was a very uncomfortable trip and we arrived about 5pm, very sore and shaken about. We set out to search for the lady who wanted us to hold meetings in her home and soon found her, because the town was not very large.

To this day, I think it will be hard to forget her name - Mrs Flea - as in the type that bite and run around under your vest! Her home was likewise, fleas everywhere. It was so infested that when we arrived back home next day I had to leave my clothes on the door-step so that they could be fumigated. We faithfully went to San Cayetano once a month - the town where Mrs Flea lived. Mostly, the only ones who came to our Bible study were children, but we trusted that some good would come out of our visits.

One month when we went Mrs Flea was not there. She had gone to Bogotá, so we sat by the road outside her house and talked to the children. Come to think of it, that time more turned up - maybe they felt less infested outside than inside. When we had finished, it was time to go and look for somewhere to stay for the night as the bus left at 4am next morning. We asked in the local café if there was a hotel and we were directed to go across the town square and there we could get a room. Not having anything else to do we went to bed early because also we had an early start next day. It was not long before it became very clear that this was maybe not the most suitable place for us to be in as it turned out to be the local brothel. The walls were made of cardboard and we had to cover our ears with a pillow. I couldn't stop laughing, but my spiritual friend was praying all night for this den of iniquity. But how were we to get out of that place next morning without being seen? It was very embarrassing and goodness knows what the people thought, these two evangelicals in the brothel!

Not long after that visit we felt it was time to go elsewhere to evangelise as it would seem that so much effort on our part was not producing much, if any, fruit. Many years later, in Zipaquirá, a young man started to come to our church. He told us that he had accepted the Lord when we visited San Cayetano. Luis later became a Pastor and married Elizabeth who lived with us. They are responsible for a large congregation of their own and are the representatives of a large county in Colombia. I sometimes wondered, in those days, if anything good was being achieved by those visits but thankfully the Lord was with us. Today I am grateful for that experience because it taught me a lot.

My years in Colombia have been a series of lessons that I have learnt - sometimes difficult ones too, often even dangerous. One such occasion made a big impression on me. I was going to go to Yakopi again (this was where I had my experience with that intoxicating fermented rice water) and Samuel was at home looking after Miriam and Martha with the help of Elizabeth. I took Sami with me and a young girl who was staying with us at the time. She was studying in Bible School in Bogotá.

We left La Palma, where we had stayed the night, very early in the morning to walk to Yakopi. We arrived at a river which I remembered having walked across easily last time but now it was a rushing torrent. So we prayed and asked the Lord to protect us. We took off our shoes and socks and started to cross the river. I went first. In between us, holding on tightly, was Sami and the young girl last. When we got to the middle of the river, suddenly a man appeared on the opposite bank and shouted to us to go not one step further. "Go back quickly", he shouted, so we did. This man appeared on horseback on our side of the river, in a few minutes. He told us that if we had taken a few more steps we would have been washed downstream because the river took away the sand where the river went round a bend, making a deep hole, which we were about to walk into. He took us upstream where we were able to cross the river, stepping on large stones, and not even our shoes got wet. Here is something to think about – was that man sent by God to protect us? I firmly believe he was. And also, when I prayed for guidance and protection after that experience, I learnt to wait for an answer and not jump in straight away.

On another occasion, going to the same place - Yakopi, I was with my son Sami and as we set off I felt a strange feeling that someone was looking at us. I was so convinced of this that I told Sami that he must stay with me, because he loved to run on ahead sometimes. We arrived at the house of the Christians and in minutes a group of men appeared. They wanted to see my identity card and what I had in my backpack. They suspected that we were American spies working with the DEA (Drug Enforcement Agency). Once they were assured we were not on any special government mission they left, but told me that they had followed us from La Palma. That was why I felt someone was looking at us – they were right behind us all the way.

I think it was on that same trip that I was asked to go and pray for healing for a believer who was sick. Well it was now getting dark, we arrived at this tiny shack and I went inside. It was pitch black, I could not see anything, but eventually I was led to a bed with a little frail very old man lying there. He must have been at least in his 80s or 90s – well, he looked very old to me. First of all I wanted to know if he was ready to meet his Lord. "Yes," he said. So I prayed. I must admit I was not really convinced that my prayer for healing had reached the Almighty. Well it seemed that it had not, because next day the old man died. They never asked me to pray for the sick again.

That trip was so memorable because in the bus on the way home, all of a sudden, everyone started hiding below the seats. Someone said we should also get down. The bus stopped and two soldiers got on and the bus moved off. Later it stopped again and the soldiers got off. In my ignorance I thought they were soldiers but they were actually from the rebel forces who kidnapped many foreigners at that time. When we got on the bus there was an old man sitting in the front seat behind the driver. When we reached our destination the driver went to wake him but he had died on the way. Two men carried him to the steps of the Catholic Church in the town square and left him there. What a trip that was! I wondered what my son thought about all this, and trusted that it had no bad effect on him. I believe that it did not because he enjoyed going on these trips and meeting the children of the Christians.

There is so much to learn about the culture and customs in Colombia. On another of the early trips to coffee country we arrived at the farm of some believers. I asked to use the toilet and I was directed to the coffee plants and was told to just hide behind any plant. So I zig-zagged through the small coffee trees and when I was sure I was well out of sight I watered one of the trees. To my horror there was a roar of laughter coming from men sitting drinking coffee. I looked round and found I was in direct line of view from the kitchen! I really learnt a lesson that day on how the coffee is planted in rows.

However, not all that happened to us in those early days was funny. Samuel visited many homes way out in the countryside and the people were always so generous, providing a meal and something to drink but often not in the most hygienic crockery.

One day, back in Zipaquirá, Samuel's skin and eyes became very yellow. So a few days later, when our missionary friends Ralph and Martha Hines came from Bogotá to visit us, Ralph took one look at Samuel and took him back to Bogotá to the clinic. Samuel had hepatitis. I was alone at home with Miriam, Sami , Martha and Elizabeth, who was about 12 years old. The next day another missionary came to take me to Bogotá because Samuel was gravely ill and the doctors were not sure if he was going to recuperate. Samuel was so sick he did not even recognise me. It was awful and very frightening. I had to return to Zipaquirá to look after the children but two days later I had to visit Samuel again because he was not getting any better but worse. When I arrived at the clinic there were four men around the bed praying for healing. Miraculously Samuel was healed, not instantly, but over quite a long period.

There was another occasion when I was ill. Samuel was in the church for the Wednesday night bible study when I had a sudden attack of asthma. I had not been ill like that since I was about 12 years old, and as I sat in bed trying to get my breath, Sami, who was about 5 years old then, woke up and came into the bedroom and asked me what was wrong. "I am sick, Sami," I said, "will you pray for me?" "OK," he said, and promptly asked the Lord to heal his mother and gave me a kiss and went back to bed. The attack of asthma soon disappeared.

After six years in Colombia I was ready for a rest. I was also expecting our fourth child. The WEC in Colombia agreed that a three months break would be good for me.

While Samuel organised the church and the farm, I set off on one of the longest trips to get to Switzerland. Miriam was now four years old and

Martha two. The cheapest way was to go to Miami first, from there to Bermuda, then on to Luxemburg and then on to Switzerland. We had to wait in Miami for about six hours for our connection. When we arrived in the airport, to my horror, Miriam lay down on the floor fascinated by the carpets. My children had not been in a home where there were these luxury items. All this was totally new to them. She was intrigued by the bathrooms too. She insisted that she needed to go about every half hour so we sat right in front of the toilets and she would take Martha there and come back together again. Once when they went yet again to the toilet they did not return for a long time. I really was worried so I asked a lady beside me to look after our luggage and went in search of my little girls. They were nowhere to be seen, then I noticed another exit door - I had thought there was only the one. There they were standing, holding tight to each other waiting to be found. I had taught them that if they were lost to always wait and not move and I would find them. Good job Miriam remembered that advice. At last we were on our way again.

My Father-in-law met us and he could see I was exhausted, so he took us to a hotel and paid for a room. Then he looked after the girls while I slept. It was so wonderful to be able to lie down on a comfortable bed, put my head on a pillow and sleep. Refreshed once more, we set off on the last part of our journey to Switzerland. We were treated to first class seats - one of my brothers–in–law had paid for us.

We stayed with my in-laws for a couple of months and then I took the girls to England where Samuel was going to join us with Sami. We were met at the airport by my Mother and Den and Vera Batt, who took us to Leigh-on-Sea where the church had provided us with a house for our time in England. I will never forget going from room to room in that wonderful place and finding so many things that the church had given us. Miriam opened a cupboard in the lounge and it was full of toys. I went to the kitchen and to my delight the cupboards and fridge were full of so many wonderful things I had not seen in years. We felt we were in paradise. I remember Martha came to ask me if she could use the table lamp by her bed. The telephone rang and the girls had no idea what it was. We had come from a happy but primitive way of living. While we were in England we enjoyed some of the luxuries too.

One night I heard the front door bell ring. I was already in bed, but looking out of the window I saw Samuel and Sami on the doorstep. I woke the girls and we went to let them in. Once more we made a tour of the house showing them all the wonderful things the church had provided. The morning after Samuel and Sami arrived in England, Sami wanted to know why I had such a big tummy. It was time to share the news that they would be having a baby brother or sister when we arrived back in Colombia. We stayed in England for about six weeks and then we went to Switzerland to be with Samuel's parents, and after two months, when I was seven months pregnant, we returned to Colombia.

Back in Colombia I began to prepare for the birth of our baby. A few days before the baby was due, I went to stay with Joy and Bill Corson in Bogotá, because they lived near to the clinic. However, day after day there was no sign that the baby was ready to be born. When I saw the doctor he decided that I should have a Caesarean section because the baby's heart beat was not very strong. So on Saturday 9th July at 4pm Suzanne came into the world. In those days (1977) there was no scan to see how the baby was or what the gender of the baby was. So I had no idea whether it would be a boy or a girl. I thought I was having a boy so we had boys' names ready but when a girl arrived we had to think again about a name. Miriam solved the problem, she said the baby should be called Suzanne, and so that was the name we gave our baby.

In 1978 Sami and Miriam started attending the Catholic school in the town, because there was no other choice for us, but the teaching standard was good. The children had to attend religious instruction classes but did not have to go to the Mass on Fridays. The religious instruction classes became a challenge but we helped them to see what the Bible said on such matters as worshiping Mary, praying for the dead, worshipping saints and many other subjects. One day Miriam told her teacher, the Nun, that it was not in the Bible that we should worship Mary. A letter came inviting Samuel to go to the school. He was not sure what to expect but to his amazement she wanted to know more about what Miriam had told her and Samuel was able to give her a small white new testament. Soon other Nuns also wanted one of those little books. The Lord works in wonderful ways.

Not so wonderful were a couple of weddings we had in the church. One was when the bridegroom did not turn up - that was very sad. The reason was that his father told him that if he married he would not pay for his university studies. This young man was a born musician and decided to run away. Two weeks later he turned up but the couple never married. On another occasion two couples decided to share the day - cheaper by the dozen maybe! The preparation went ahead and all was organised for the grand day. One couple would bring the cake and the others would decorate the church. One couple arrived at the church in time but there was no sign of the other couple. So after waiting half an hour or more, singing choruses all the time, Samuel decided to go ahead anyway. I stood at the door to indicate when the others arrived. Half way through the service I saw the man coming along with a parcel under his arm and then I noticed the lady on the other side of the road also with a bundle under her arm. The man explained that they would not be getting married after all, but after I talked with them they decided to go ahead. So I rushed the lady to a friend's house and while she got dressed I made her a bouquet of flowers from the friend's garden. We hurried to the church where Samuel had to start all over again!

Two months later couple number two stood on our doorstep telling us that they wanted a divorce. It came out that the lady had a son who was nine years old and the boy had always slept with his mother and in no way was allowing this new guy into his mother's bed. The boy came to stay with us for a few days while a "honeymoon" took place, and we explained to the lad that there was to be a change in the home. Thankfully he accepted it and they made him a nice bedroom too.

Once, we took in someone who had some mental health issues – he had walked miles to come and visit Samuel. He was taken to the hospital but a few days later, when Samuel went past the place, this fellow had escaped and was jumping from the top of one car to another, all belonging to doctors. Samuel left quickly in case they charged him with the damage. Another time two Swiss tourists arrived at the farm with a big snake in a box – it was a huge snake. We let these young men stay for a while but when the snake escaped one night I could stand it no longer. The snake was duly captured and the young men dispatched.

Chapter 12 – Troubled Years

Once more we faced another challenge. This time it was that we should go further afield to evangelise. Samuel decided to prepare a group of people to go with him to open up a church in Barranquilla on the north coast of Colombia. At that time it took three days to get there because the roads were so bad. Every Wednesday they met to prepare for this trip in prayer, bible study and methods of evangelism. The whole church was involved one way or another.

We collected various articles ready for the big day when they would be going far away. There was a need for camp beds, hammocks, rice, beans, bibles, literature, and various other items. Those of us who stayed at home pledged to pray and keep in touch. It really was very difficult for those who went as the majority had never been any further than the city and on the coast it is a very different culture. Our people were on a missionary journey to places unknown to them.

When their letters began to arrive telling of their experiences, they told of extreme heat, and of a people who enjoyed lively music - their way of life was very different. The team had permission from another denomination to stay at an existing church. A survey was made and when they found an area where there was no other church, they moved in order to start a work there. They rented a house, and prayer and meetings began. The work grew quickly and after about two months Samuel came back to Zipaquirá, leaving a capable young man in charge. When the group was large enough I went to help organise and prepare people to work with the children, of which there were so many. I found it so hard to understand what the local people were saying – they had a different dialect and also spoke very quickly. The people on the coast were very friendly and open to learn anything new. Soon it was possible to let the team continue on their own and after two years, when the work was well established, we handed the church over to the Colombian Pastors who then took charge. Another team of volunteers from Zipaquirá were prepared and they went to the next town, St. Martha, also on the coast - and so the work grew.

Sometimes where there is blessing one also experiences opposition and we went through a very difficult time with our neighbours. For some unknown reason the farmer who owned land next to ours decided to put up extra fences on a public path which ran in between our farms. This was very inconvenient and also illegal. Samuel consulted the town council and they said we were to use the path and not allow it to be closed by the farmer. One day, when Samuel went that way and he had Miriam and Sami with him, the man came at Samuel with a huge stick and hit him near his neck and a huge bruise appeared. With an aching head it was necessary to go to the police because he was almost knocked out. The man was warned not to do that again which he obeyed but one night, when Samuel went down to the church for a meeting, this crazy farmer started to shoot at our house. Every time I put a light on in any room a shot was fired. I was very worried about Samuel because as he came walking home he would have no idea what danger he was in. The man could see Samuel from his vantage point above our house. So I crept round the house putting on lights and each time a shot went whizzing overhead. I thought maybe in that way he would use up all his ammunition. At last I saw Samuel coming up the path and I yelled at him to be very careful because the neighbour had a gun. Fortunately the man had got tired or there were no more bullets left.

Problems like these, and some were more violent than others, were very difficult for me to manage. I began to wonder why the Lord didn't intervene and help us. During 1979 - 1980 I went through a very difficult time. When Samuel was away visiting the churches I had so much to do.

I was responsible for the church, running the farm and looking after the family.

One Saturday, while I was in the kitchen, I heard the loud speaker, which the town council used to inform the people about local events, say that in the afternoon it was organised that everyone should get a machete and take their dogs up to the foreigners farm and to cut up all the hosepipes because we were supposedly stealing water from the people. This was just not true. Samuel had actually built a special tank so that the people had more water, but they forgot that fact and sure enough, in the afternoon, I saw them coming.

I had the children with me in the kitchen and there was no-one nearby to help me. The workers had Saturday afternoon free until milking time. I began praying, "Lord do not let them come into the farm," and they advanced. "Lord please don't let them come to the stable," and they came. "Lord help me, don't let them come onto the patio outside the window," and they came. They were shouting at us. It was terrifying. They then started to cut up any pipe they found. When everything was in turmoil they left. My children were crying at my feet, I was shaking, and then a worker appeared and we went to look at the damage. I had no water for the house, nor for the cows at milking time, nor in the field where they were that day. There was no water anywhere on the farm.

My questions began: "Lord I needed you. How come, here I am serving you and when I need help you are silent." Why was the Lord not on my side anymore? The Lord was still on my side but I was not hearing because I was not spending time with Him. I began to doubt many things. I was really tired and seemed to have no time for myself and even less to pray and study the Bible. This was a dangerous situation to be in spiritually.

However, in between the negative incidents some amazing things happened too. One Sunday, when we were going to get ready for church, we noticed that part of the forest was on fire. There had been no rain and the ground was covered in dry leaves and the fire was spreading quickly. There was no fire brigade in our town or even nearby. Samuel got the workers together to go and put the fire out. I went down to the town to our church to start a prayer time. The sky was clear blue, not a cloud was in sight, but we prayed to the Lord and someone suddenly called out, "Look!" A big black cloud had appeared and it began to rain right over the town and our farm and the fire was put out. When we arrived home we heard another amazing story. They were fighting the fire and suddenly Samuel found himself surrounded by flames, he had no way out without getting burnt and then the rain came and he was free to walk away.

At this time, with four children to bring up, a marriage to keep alive, a church to maintain, and many demands crowding in on any spare time, I was often stretched to my limits. That is how I felt in 1980. I really was worn out and there was a lot of pressure on me. I also was very lonely – my husband was hardly ever at home. I had no real friends with whom I could share my problems. The Pastor's wife is often a lonely person and it is difficult to unwind and relax. I began also to doubt the Lord. Why did I sense that my prayers were not being answered? I was frustrated. We had been through a set of problems with the neighbours and the rebel forces were constantly on our tails too.

Three elements which are not helpful are: being tired, having some medical problem and not spending time alone with the Bible. This was my situation, and I did not know what to do with all that. I began to cry all the time, there were so many things I just could not face. I just wanted to curl up and go to sleep until all this was past.

The missionaries became aware of my state and it was suggested that a three months break would do me good. I was in such a bad way emotionally by now that even looking after the children became difficult. So Samuel decided to send our two eldest children to Switzerland to his parents. That was awful - I felt so dreadful letting them go and of course they could not understand what was happening to us all. Now it was my turn to travel, with Martha who was five and Suzanne, who was three years old. We went straight to England because I had to undergo surgery at Mildmay hospital.

I arrived at Heathrow really worn out by the journey. My mother was there to meet us and I just let her take over. The church once more provided us with a house and that was very helpful. However, I sank deeper into depression and I was in a very bad way when I went to London to see a doctor. The doctor had been a missionary in Africa for many years and, thankfully, he could see what I was going through. After a short physical examination he then took a long time talking to me. His final words were a shock. I could no longer return to Colombia as my emotional state was not able to cope with any pressure. He said that never again was I to go back under any circumstances. My first thoughts were "Whatever will Samuel say?" The doctor said he would tell my husband when he arrived in England.

Samuel arrived a day or two before I went into hospital for an operation that I needed. He was also devastated. His love for Colombia and the people was so great he could not imagine never going back there. That time was very difficult for both of us.

After recuperating from the operation we went to Switzerland to meet up with the children. I never imagined it was possible to go through what we had to experience in the coming months. If I felt that the Lord was distant before, now He was totally missing, or so I felt. Sami and

Miriam had been through a difficult time too. They were put in school just a week after they arrived in Switzerland and did not know one word of Swiss. We had always felt it best for the children speak Spanish to help them with their education. Can you imagine their confusion?

We went straight to my in-laws home to stay there until something could be worked out. What a time! Sami and Miriam had been in Switzerland for some four months and were now only speaking Swiss, so Martha and Suzanne could not understand what they were on about. It was chaos. But somehow we lived through it, and one day something good happened and we were offered an apartment in the building where my brother-in-law was house parent in a children's home. It was only for a short time but we could live there until it was needed for a couple who would later work in the home.

This was wonderful, we were on our own, and we had all we needed, even food from the home. The place was fully furnished and warm and comfortable. At last we felt that something was working for our good. We lived there some nine months and in that time Samuel had to go to Colombia to sort out some problems on the farm and try to sell it.

We were getting along somehow but no-one knew what to do with me to help me, but kept telling me that a rest and time would heal me. So I hoped, but going back to Colombia was not to be. I think, at the time, I was secretly glad not to go back. We were enjoying many good times where we were. The children made friends and enjoyed taking part in all the activities that the home offered. In summer they learnt to swim; when winter came they learnt to ski and enjoyed the winter sports too. Christmas came and went and I thought we were now settled when my brother-in –law told us that he needed the apartment, and in a week's time. My father–in–law had been searching for a place to live for us but nothing had turned up - now we were desperate. It seemed that the

Lord wanted to show us He was still around because in one week we saw so many amazing things happen.

On the Monday Samuel went to a prayer meeting and met a school friend from many years ago. He told him we needed somewhere to live. The friend said that a place had just become free right where he was living. Next day all was settled, we had somewhere to live, but we had not one stick of furniture, no linen - actually we had nothing.

On the Tuesday a friend phoned me to say her mother had gone into a home and she had all her linen if we should ever need some. It was sent to the new place we had, and so it went on all week, every day someone offered us something for our apartment.

It was amazing! We went on the Saturday and found boxes and furniture, food, kitchen supplies, a gas stove, dining room furniture, and even the bedrooms fitted out. It was better than Christmas! That night we all slept in super beds with fresh clean linen, food in our stomachs and peace and happiness seemed to flow among us once more.

On the following Monday I said to Samuel that the only things missing now were cleaning utensils. We planned to buy what was needed next day, but in the afternoon of that same day a missionary friend phoned telling us that he was leaving for Africa in a few days and was wondering if we could use their hoover, mops, and brooms, among other things. That was another surprise for us.

Sometime later, an old lady who knew Samuel for many years telephoned and asked him if he could visit her. Later he came home with a big surprise - standing outside the house was a green Renault 4, a gift from that dear lady!

During this time I often found myself feeling guilty because I thought all the upheaval and difficulties we were having were entirely my fault. I constantly accused myself, time and time again, but that did not bring any solution. Some days were better than others and I tried to make this time as happy as possible for the children and my husband. Some days I found help reading the Psalms; it was great to see that David often felt like I did. Reading Psalm 39 became my help because I could identify with David - he too was desperately looking for help and guidance. One night I remember crying out to the Lord, "How long, Lord?" All I seemed to get was silence but actually the Lord was there, and one day we really saw His help in a practical way which encouraged me a lot.

It was on a Wednesday when we really hit a low spot because there was no money and no food. The children had the afternoon free and so we went out for a walk taking a plastic bag with us to collect any fallen apples we might find on the way. Walking actually gave us more of an appetite. When we arrived home, to our surprise, there was a huge black plastic bag at our door. We quickly went inside the apartment to see what was in the bag. It was full of food - tins of fruit, packets of soup, pasta, rice, biscuits, chocolate and many other delightful things to eat. Right at the bottom of the bag was an envelope with money inside. We had no idea who had given us that very special bag of food that day but it really was such a help to me in restoring some hope.

Many weeks later a dear old lady who prayed for us regularly told us the story. She was praying for us one morning when she kept thinking about what she would have for lunch that day. It bothered her that she could not concentrate on her prayer time so she got up and went to her kitchen cupboard to set aside her lunch and then continue praying for us. When she was in the kitchen she suddenly thought, "What if the Bernhard's have no food for today?" So she started to fill a plastic bag with things she thought we might need and put some money in an envelope too. The Lord was with us after all! Often we think we are on our own but with this example we can see that He has a watching eye on us all the time and knows the exact moment when we need help, and supplies it.

Time went by. We somehow got on with life, waiting to know what our future was to be like, until one day a Swiss couple telephoned to ask if they could come and talk to us about Colombia. They came one Saturday afternoon. I served them coffee and prepared to take the children to the park, mostly because when I found out that they were going to Colombia and wanted to know if Samuel would accompany them I did not want to be part of the conversation.

As I said goodbye to excuse myself, the lady said, "Wait, Janet. I think you need some help. I am a Christian Counsellor and I want to help you." I could hardly believe what I was hearing. She actually noticed I was going through a very difficult time and she could help me. So far no-one had offered. I sat down and cried but this time in relief. Charlotte Bruderer took out her diary and said she would come every Saturday until I was free from so much pain and confusion. Yes, she did come and she took me through a number of sessions. Some weeks later there was a change and I believed at last that the Lord was healing me again. There was freedom from so many situations in the past that were hindering me. I began to understand what had caused the trouble. It was a series of circumstances which had accumulated. Having attended many women who had very difficult situations in their lives, I felt it was my responsibility to solve their problems. Since that time I have learnt differently and I have learnt that the person needs to see that Christ has the answer, and my privilege is to lead that person to Him and the Bible.

Another problem area was that I had no-one to talk to about the difficulties we had with the neighbours, the rebel forces and many other issues. I found no outlet and so the difficult times began to be stored up inside me. On top of that, I was very tired and worn out and needed a minor operation. The way that Charlotte helped me was in writing. I wrote down all my fears, and then recognising that Jesus Christ came to this earth, lived among us and knows my anxieties. He alone can, and is, the only one who takes away my desperation when I ask Him to. Session after session I learnt to unwind and let go of so many hurts of emotional pain. I was free one step at a time.

We contacted the WEC and went to the headquarters to talk to our leaders. I had to see those in England too for their approval for my return to Colombia. Samuel and I met up with them in Switzerland, and at that meeting one more step came in my healing process. Neil Rowe prayed for me and he quoted Joshua 1 v 5: "No man shall be able to stand before you all the days of your life; as I was with Moses so I shall be with you, I will not fail you or forsake you".

There are wonderful promises in that verse. Neil also read other verses which became my help - as was Isaiah 41 v 8–14. Then also he read from the Psalms. These were the words I needed to hear and believe in order to be able to go back to the same problems or worse and be able to cope, this time knowing that the Lord was always on my side and He had the answers.

During my times with Charlotte I realised that when I went to Colombia there was an idea that it was my duty to go to serve the Lord. I thought that my DUTY would see me through, but during the process she took me through I saw that there was a vital factor missing. One of the leaders of WEC prayed for me just before we returned to Colombia. He prayed that I would sense the Lord's love flow through me. The promises began to come to mind: "I will never leave you nor forsake you". I remembered that there was a promise which said, "I will be with you wherever you go". Another one came to mind: "I love you with an everlasting love and will be with you." Somehow I sensed a new assurance that the Lord was with me, that I need not fear, and that He loved me. I also realised that I had been serving the Lord with the wrong motive. It was His love I needed to keep me going, and to share with the Colombians and anyone else who came my way looking for help. I found and sensed something very real had taken place in me. I can honestly say that I went back to Colombia with a different attitude, no longer because of a duty, but because of His love flowing through me to people. I also went to London to meet the Doctor who had seen me at the beginning of my troubles and he too was amazed how the Lord had healed my emotions and that I was now free to return to Colombia.

Before we actually went back we had to wait some time while this process was taking place. We were very cramped in that small apartment so we managed to move to another town and lived in a house for a while before packing everything up once more. In this same period it was necessary for Samuel to return to Colombia to organise the children's schooling and talk with the Colombian Pastors. We lost count how many times we moved! The good part was that we became experts in packing up and unpacking. We could move out and into a new place, and that same night everyone was in their own bed, their clothes in the closet and the table set for tomorrow's breakfast! That is not to say the children enjoyed all this, for them it was very difficult and to this day most of the four hate the prospect of having to move.

Once more, in August 1983, we packed up the house and said good-bye to our family and friends and went to England on our journey back to Colombia.

Chapter 13 - Returning to Colombia

In July 1983 the children finished school and we were on our way back to Colombia. In some ways this was victory, but with some apprehension on my part. Now it was time to prove the reality - if what I had experienced would really work in practice.

As soon as the children knew we were going back there were two reactions. One was that some stability would now help us all. Not knowing for so long what our future would be had caused a lot of insecurity. Then when they knew there would be no more skiing, no winter sports, again leaving the friends they had made, and picking up with the ones in Colombia, that brought its own difficulties but we had to go ahead and trust the Lord for all these details.

This was not an easy time. Once more we had to leave family and friends behind to return to the place that the Lord had called us to serve Him. All these changes and moving around, plus sometimes not even understanding what the Lord was doing - this is often part of the missionary's life.

We arrived at the airport in Bogotá to a big surprise because there was a crowd of friends who had come to welcome us back. That was so special, to know that the people were so glad that we had returned after two and a half years away. We went to Zipaquirá and woke up next morning to familiar surroundings, in our home again. We assisted at the church which was now pastored by a friend of ours. The plan was for us to go to live in Bogotá where Samuel would be working with the Colombian church, visiting and helping wherever he was needed. While we searched for a house, and the children adapted once more to Spanish, we stayed some three months in Zipaquirá.

One day I noticed, while looking out of the window, that on the land next to our farm some building was now in progress. It seemed to me that the work had started overnight because I had not been aware of it before. One day a lady from the church asked me if I was nervous about the new neighbours. My answer was that I saw no reason to be nervous, until she told me who these people were. It happened that the rebel forces, known as the M19 (a terrifying group of men), had literally taken the land by force from the owner one night and were building a shanty town right on our doorstep. This news absolutely shocked me. One of my biggest fears was that any member of our family, including me, might be kidnapped. This had been one of my problems, one reason I had to go home. It was happening right here on our doorstep. "Lord, not again!" I cried out. I went to our bedroom and on my knees asked the Lord why was He putting me in this situation when we had only just arrived back. In the silence that followed some verses came to mind.

Isaiah 41 v 9 – 14: "You who I took from the ends of the earth, and called from the far corners, saying to you - you are my servant, I have chosen you and not cast you off; fear not, for I am with you, be not dismayed, for I am your God; I will strengthen you, I will help you, I will uphold you with my right hand."

Then another verse came into my mind, Joshua 1 v 5: "No man shall be able to stand before you all the days of your life, as I was with Moses so I shall be with you." And Jeremiah 31 v 3: "I love you with an everlasting love, I will be with you". My beating heart began to calm down, assurance came, and then I remembered a phrase I had heard a long time before - sometimes the Lord takes us back to the place where we lost a battle in order to show us that now there was victory. Yes, there was victory and with these promises I would carry on.

Once more we were on the move. In January we began to look for a house in Bogotá. One day we saw a place in a street where there was a guard at the entrance for safety - this is normal. The buildings were new but the only one left was small and tucked in between two houses. Then, on a corner in the same road, I saw a place which was more suitable for us. Fortunately we were able to move later in the month.

What a wonderful feeling to move into a brand new house - finished and all in working order. The Lord was guiding. We moved once more, and the children began school in January. Life was taking on a stable routine. We attended a nearby church of the same denomination with our friends Ruth and Antonio Cortes. Samuel helped with the preaching and carried on visiting and helping churches which were passing through some difficulty. I began in the Sunday school. We were now settled once more and it was wonderful to be active and proving the faithfulness of God in our lives - and then suddenly we were thrown into another crisis.

One morning our son Sami, now 13 years old, complained of a pain in his right arm. Later, when the pain got worse and he began to have a high temperature which would not go down, we took him to the hospital. He was placed on a trolley and was waiting to see a doctor when one passed by and then came back. He asked what was wrong and then examined our son. He said that Sami had sceptic rheumatism, which was very dangerous - he must not be moved on any account. The doctor had to go to Bogotá to operate but would be back at 3 o'clock to operate on our son. Sure enough at 3 o'clock the operation began. We prayed and called friends to join us in prayer. I had to go to Bogotá to collect some clothes for Sami and some medical papers. When I arrived at our house and began putting together what I needed, it came to my mind that in all circumstances we should praise the Lord, but surely not at a time like this? But it became clear to me that I was to praise the Lord. So with great difficulty I began to sing and praise the Lord.

Later, when I arrived back at the hospital, Sami was recovering, but the doctor told us that the next 24 hours were crucial and if his temperature did not come down he would have to amputate his arm. We prayed so fervently, and what wonderful news next day to hear that, yes, his temperature had come down and he was recuperating well. Poor lad, he was in a room with some men, but they were looking after him and were all so kind, although Sami felt uncomfortable with the statues of Saints which were placed around the room. The Catholic nurses who attended him were so kind too. At visiting time the room was filled with our son's friends who had come from Bogotá to see him. A couple of days later we took him home. He was getting stronger every day. The only problem was that the wound would not close up - it just would not heal. So many ointments and remedies were recommended to us but in the end the only one that worked was to wrap some raw sugar in a bandage - called "panela" in Spanish - scraped from a block and placed around the arm at night. This home remedy worked!

I wonder if you can believe it - once more we were on the move! We were like Nomads. After a while I lost count of just how many times we moved in those years.

It was 1987 and, one Sunday, Samuel was looking in the paper and said that after church we would go and look at a house which, according to the advert, was a "Swiss-style house". So after church we went to look at that house but at first we could not find it, and then all of a sudden we saw a house which did look very Swiss. To our amazement there was a notice in the window saying it was for sale. We rang the bell and, another surprise, the lady who came to answer was a veterinary doctor who Samuel had met once or twice. We looked round the house and absolutely fell in love with it. So the price was asked and then we realised the one big drawback - they wanted the money in cash and in one lump sum. That was out of the question for us.

So sadly we left but dreamed on. Back at home over lunch we rearranged our furniture in that new house. We made plans, such as who would have which bedroom - even though it seemed hopeless. For nine months we pestered and asked that lady about the house. We felt that house was now ours as we had dreamt so much about it! Well, the following Sunday Samuel said we would go one last time. We waited for the lady to answer the door and we thought that she was surprised to see us.

On Saturday night she had telephoned her brother, who was actually the owner but who now lived in Sweden, and told him that the only people who came with money were those who were laundering drug money. The brother was tired of this continuous problem, so he said that the first people who came with a suitable offer, give it to them, and we were the first to come and ask!

You may remember in the early pages of this book, when I told about how much I always wanted a dolls house and my Dad said, "When I can give you one I will do so, but you must be patient." Here I was once more wanting, but this time it was a real house and the Lord said, "Be patient, when I can I will give it to you." The lesson was learnt long ago and now put into practice.

We moved in a couple of weeks later!

Chapter 14 – Building a New Church

Life is full of new beginnings and for our family a new chapter began for us too.

I remember one day, soon after we moved into our new house, Samuel stood in front of the fireplace downstairs in the lounge and said, "We could begin a church in this place." That came to pass. In October, in our home, we began a prayer time with a small group of friends asking the Lord for guidance. We were attending the church of the Christian Crusade where the Pastors were our friends Ruth and Antonio Cortes. It was agreed that we should begin a church in the area where we lived because, on checking, we found that in and around our home there was no evangelical witness.

At first we met for prayer, and then afterwards we would walk the streets near the house praying for our neighbours, that we would be able to bring them to Christ. The official opening was in March 1988, but the group grew so quickly we had to find somewhere else because we could not fit everyone into our dining room and lounge, although they were quite big. We had an interesting way of inviting people to our bible studies and prayer times. On Friday evening, now and then, each couple would bring another couple for a meal, and during that time we would talk about how each one of us had come to know the Lord. This brought many to join with us as we walked together in the Christian life.

The church grew and once more it was necessary to find a bigger place. We moved twice in two years and the last place was suitable to expand, right there on the site. We bought a house with an enormous garden. The house became the offices, book store, Pastor's office, kitchen for coffee after the meetings and for fellowship and a chat. We built the meeting hall in the garden which eventually held over 600 people.

Much later we bought the house next to the church when it came on the market - that area became our Junior Church. It had a bigger kitchen and had a fireplace where we had some special times chatting round the fire. The house also had a large garden which was used a lot for the children's work. The Lord blessed and prospered that time in the life of the church and in our lives too.

In 1986 I went to England, to visit my church in Leigh–on-Sea to give them an up-date on what we were doing in Colombia, to visit the different organisations in the church and meet with prayer groups, because our work in Colombia was not just us. We had a large team of people in England who faithfully prayed for the work in Colombia. I stayed with my mother and went to various friends also. My mother had lived by herself for some 14 years and she visited us in Colombia twice, I believe. She was a great help in keeping our friends up-to-date with the Lord's work in Colombia. On that occasion, near the end of my visit, a friend from the church (Reg Lewis) offered me a lift to the station. In the car park he asked me to pray for a wife for him because, since his wife had died, he was very lonely. So I prayed. Very soon after I arrived back in Colombia I received a telegram from my mother announcing that she was going to marry Reg Lewis in a couple of weeks. What a surprise! This is how it happened. The Sunday after I left for Colombia Reg saw my mother sitting on her own in Church so he invited her to have coffee with him after the evening service. I am told that they chatted for hours. Next day Reg took my mother out for the day in his car. She loved car rides. Tuesday he proposed to her. Wednesday they bought the ring. Thursday they set the date with the Minister. Friday she sent the telegram and Reg told his son Paul that he was getting married in a couple of weeks, but he would not say who he was marrying. Paul and Mary, his wife, looked through the church directory and thought that maybe the most suitable woman was my mother - she was the lucky one.

They were married in 1986. I became the step-sister to Paul. Imagine, at 47 years old I was given a step-brother! Reg and my mother were together for three and a half very happy years, until my mother died. I went to England for the funeral, which was a sad time for all of us. I packed up my mother's things and took some of her precious treasures with me back to Colombia. Reg was heartbroken - dear man.

My Mother was 75 years old and Reg was nearing his 80th birthday when they married. When he wrote to tell me they were getting married, and so quickly after meeting up for coffee, he said, "Janet, at our age not a day can be wasted." They lived every day to the full, not wasting one day.

In the meantime the congregation grew under Samuel's good guidance as he prepared leaders and Pastors for the work. I began preparing a new idea for the children's work. In Leigh Road Baptist Church I had seen how they did Sunday school and I realised that we were way behind in our methods with the children. It was called "J Team" but it took a couple of years to organise and get it all ready. It was necessary to train teachers and prepare properly for this project.

At the same time our family was preparing for the future and our children were in University or studying in some capacity for the future. About this time I decided I wanted to go away for a personal retreat, to be alone with the Lord. I also wanted to know that the Lord was with me, even on my own. Samuel took me to a place in the country where I was very much alone. It was a lovely house with a fireplace, a stove to do my cooking on and heated with firewood. There was no electricity and a long way away from any other houses. It was so special. I had my dog with me, a black Labrador. In the evening I had my radio with batteries, classical music, a good book and all by candle-light.

One night I was in bed and I heard heavy steps outside. I froze. I usually fear the worst in any situation, and this was no different. My instant thought was that the rebels have come for me. I was shaking in bed and thought, "Well, I may die here of a heart attack but maybe it is nothing serious." With great courage I got out of bed and opened the window. It turned out to be a cow eating the flowers - I had forgotten to close the gate!

Later in the week, though, I had a strange sensation that I was being watched in the afternoons. My dog barked looking in one direction but I saw no-one. By Sunday I was glad that Samuel was coming to collect me next morning, to take me back to Bogotá. When he came and I told him I had not seen the farm hand, who works there, for a few days. He went in search of him and came back in a hurry. He told me to pack up as quickly as possible - we had to leave right now. I was very puzzled by this news but Samuel would not say why. We left and arrived in Bogotá the quickest I have ever known. Samuel called a friend who came and they talked in low tones together. Whatever was going on? Samuel said it was best for me not to know, but that was worse than ever. So he told me that just behind the house there were five rebels waiting for him, to kidnap him. They obviously did not want me. They had been there for four days and that was why the farm hand had vanished. The Lord had once more protected me and kept me from harm.

We used to go to a place in the country where we could relax. Once, early one morning, we went to spend the day there. When we arrived the farm hand was amazed to see us. He had been trying to contact Samuel to tell him not to come because on the way there were two different roads we could take and on both of those roads were stationed two different rebel groups, both kidnapping people on their way to their farms.

We wondered how should we go back, which road to take? Both were equally dangerous. How we had gone so far and had no problem was, in itself, a miracle. So we began our journey with a lot of fear and prayer. After a very short time a terrible storm struck and the rain came down so hard that the windscreen wipers failed. Eventually we arrived safely in the next town. What a relief. We sat in the car and thanked the Lord for keeping us and Samuel said, "I believe that the rain was sent to protect us – the rebels don't like getting wet!"

In 1995 we had our silver wedding anniversary and to celebrate we had a fancy dress party. Samuel dressed in his wedding suit and I wore my wedding dress but with a wide piece of red satin in a gap in the back of my dress. It was great fun. Samuel loved to be the actor and dress up. He was King Herod at Christmastime in the play they did each year in the church. Or he was a street person on another occasion and, at a meal for the leaders, no-one knew it was Samuel wearing a wig, standing at the door with a cup in his hand, begging. Worse than that, no-one took compassion on him!

By 1997 the church was very blessed. We had three services on Sunday, a large young people's group, four part-time pastors and many leaders, all trained and prepared. Our days were full and it was time again to reach out to other areas around us and further afield too. A new church was set up as a daughter church further out of town. Later a couple felt the Lord was leading them to go to the USA, to Boca Raton, to start a work there among an Hispanic group.

Also about this time Samuel was chosen to go to Hawaii to the course given by the Haggai Institute. With expenses paid, he set off with great expectations about this time far away. It was an amazing experience meeting so many chosen men from different parts of the world. He came back on fire, to carry on serving the Lord.

By 1998 the church had been established ten years and we had been in Colombia since 1971. The church in Zipaquirá and all the others were now under the guidance of the National Church. We were responsible for the churches which were daughter churches of the one in Cedritos, Bogotá.

The world was preparing to celebrate the year 2000. We read of amazing and exotic ways you could spend millions of pounds, so that you would never forget the year 2000. Our church in England invited us to go there in 2001 to celebrate God's good hand on us and to praise Him for the work set up in Colombia. But before that, we would never forget the year 1999.

Chapter 15 - Forgiveness

In 1999, and for the next ten years, our family went through the most awful and sad situations. Our faith was put on trial and our confidence in the Lord stretched to the limits. We, as a family, went through three divorces, three premature babies died, we had serious health problems, several robberies, moral principles were shattered, and changes which I never thought possible in a million years - all this happened to us.

At the time it is easy to think, "When I get to heaven I have a few questions to ask the Lord." What mortal silly questions! When we get there we will be so thrilled to meet the Lord face to face, all this will never even be thought about, but we do have questions. What went wrong? Why us? Who is to blame? And so the questions go on and on and of course with no real answers. We really felt shattered and the worst was yet to come. How was it possible that the Bernhard family had passed through so many difficult times? What went wrong?

One Sunday in 2003 I opened that email from my husband and he told me he did not want to carry on living with me. I spent many sleepless nights and endless days with a thousand and one questions in my head. When we are low in spirits the enemy enjoys playing with our thoughts. It was so difficult to know what to do and who to turn to. In the beginning, WEC International did all they could to help me and to try to get Samuel to join me in Switzerland, where help was available for us both. But my husband was adamant and no-one could convince him to try and sort something out.

I was at a stage in life when I felt grateful for all the Lord had enabled me to do. I was a grandmother, my children were all professionals, and the church work had progressed so well. I imagined a new stage in life with my husband and maybe a different ministry, perhaps as advisors now, and being able to take life with a bit less action. We had been married, at this time, for 32 years. What happened to Samuel? Only he knows, I cannot answer for him but it was so difficult to understand. My husband was a faithful servant of the Lord; he was our family's leader and we looked up to him. He had led so many people to the Lord and into the ministry too. He was a man of vision and the Lord guided him and prospered him in all he did. He was also admired and recognised in many Christian circles. The danger to go a different way is always there. Temptation lurks around every corner and we, all of us, must be on guard all the time, but with the Lord's help we can resist if we want to.

After the initial shock I had questions, "What is my future in all this, Lord? What will my happen to me now?" But amazingly, looking back, this was a very special time for me spiritually.

Many people came with different advice, prophecies, and guidance from God. There were accusations and their personal opinions as to what I should do. All this was very confusing. I also felt very much alone and many people could not understand what had happened and were confused. So, rather than get involved, they left me alone. I soon realised I had to rely on the Lord only, for Him to guide me. My relationship with the Lord grew and I found guidance from the Bible in my daily readings.

In the first weeks after this news, many emails went back and forth but it was obvious there would be no change of mind. I was in Switzerland and I was advised to stay for a while. The mission was doing its best to help Samuel and me, but my living conditions were rather inconvenient. I was living with Miriam and Ali, her husband, with their baby, Daniel. One Tuesday night when I could not sleep, at about 3 am I prayed: "Lord, I need somewhere to live, nearby, and the money to live with."

On the Thursday of that same week, the leaders of WEC Switzerland came to visit me and as they were leaving they asked me where I was going to live. I told them I had prayed about that on Tuesday night. My reading at the time was Psalm 23 verse 2-3: "The Lord is my shepherd, I shall not want, He makes me to lie down in green pastures, He leads me beside still waters, He restores my soul." They had an amazing answer. Some friends of the mission had offered a furnished flat. It was situated ten minutes away from Lake Zurich and I only had to pay for the electricity and the usual services that I used. This was truly of the Lord. That couple became my friends and they were amazing in showing so much love and help.

Here were my green pastures and still waters, and in that place the Lord began restoring my soul. A few days later I opened my mail. I was now somewhat cautious about opening emails. A note told me that my church in England would give me a financial gift each month to help me. That is just the beginning of a thousand and one ways the Lord took me through the coming months, and now years.

Time went by, nothing changed in the situation and my life took on a new routine, which helped. For three days in the week I looked after Daniel while Miriam was at work and Ali was studying for his Master's degree in Architecture in Zurich.

Then on the other days Ali took over and I went to Rapperswil where the apartment, which had been loaned to me, was located. I will hopefully never forget the kindness shown to me by the owners of that apartment. Sometimes I found a lovely bowl of fruit in the kitchen. Then on other occasions an invitation came for a meal with Rene and Walter Kagi. They lived just downstairs. The months came and went, and it was time to make a decision about the next step. Miriam and Ali, with baby Daniel, were going back to Colombia so I decided it would be good to go with them. So on 11th July 2004, which happened to be my wedding anniversary, we were on the plane back to Colombia.

The day before we travelled my daily reading from the bible was in Deuteronomy 31 verse 8: "It is the Lord who goes before you; He will be with you, He will not fail you or forsake you; do not fear or be dismayed." I was very nervous about what would happen next. It had been arranged beforehand that my friends Betty and Hans Muller would take me to their home first so that I could adjust to life in Colombia and work out, from a distance, when it would be the right time to return to our house.

Most days I was on my own as the family all went to school and the office. Now and then Samuel would come and visit, sometimes with promises which were never fulfilled. I received so much help from the family I was staying with and it was amazing how the Lord put people in my path to shelter me and provide for me.

However, every now and then the dark days were there, and when I knew I had to return to the house and live in the same place as Samuel, my heart broke once more.

To be so near and yet so far was a torture. When it got hard I used to put on a CD of Christian music and sing my heart out. That really helped. I was there in that situation when, in September, Samuel began telling me the divorce papers were nearly ready. However in the world was I going to sign something which was completely against my principals? Lord, whatever shall I do?

I consulted three friends who were mature Christians and leaders and individually they all said there was no way out and that Samuel would not change his position. I set aside three days to pray about this most difficult step of divorce. After two days I knew I had to go through with it and the Lord knew my heart and my pain, but it was the only way through. In October the fateful day came. It was terrible to sit in that Registry Office and sign those papers, with my husband sitting at the same table. Next day Samuel left the house for good.

The coming days and weeks were awful, and I fell into times of not even desiring to live. One day I was still in bed at 11 o'clock and wanting the Lord to do me the favour and take me. Whatever was the reason to live? This was the end of my missionary career, and to finish like this? I saw no way out. But then I remembered that I had not read my Bible in three days so, reluctantly, I told the Lord, "I really am only doing this because I have not read Your Word for a while and maybe I should."

At the time I was reading through the Psalms and the reading for the day was Psalm 46:

Verses 1-2: "God is our refuge and strength a very present help in trouble. Therefore we will not fear though the earth should change, though the mountains shake in the heart of the sea."

Verse 5: "God is in the midst of her, she shall not be moved; God will help her at break of day."

Verse 10: "Be still and know that I am God; I will be exalted among the nations; I will be exalted in the earth."

Verse 11: "The Lord of hosts is with us, the God of Jacob is our refuge."

I got out of bed, really amazed at what I had read. I stood by the window and said to the Lord: "Lord, we will fight this together and with your help I will not allow the devil to win in my life. One of us has taken another road but, Lord, You and I will be a testimony to show how You can restore and renew a broken heart and put my feet on firm ground. Today, Lord, is a new beginning for me, with You at my side I will conquer what lies ahead. Lord, I want to be a testimony of how You can renew a life and use it once more."

My help came from the Lord, constantly. The days that were ahead of me were far from easy but never again did I have that desire to ask the Lord to take me and, as you can see, He did not answer that prayer!

The next step in my emotional healing, I think, was about forgiving. Forgiving is a crisis of our will. To be willing to forgive allows God to touch the centre of our emotions. Forgiving is the only way to be free and stop the resentment. To forgive sets me free from the constant reminder of what has happened. It also sets the other person free to be blessed. To forgive stops the desire for revenge. Oh yes, I read all this in various books and especially on a course I did in WEC Washington DC, USA on counselling. However, it is one thing putting that into my mind and another putting it into practice.

As time went by I began to see that not to forgive was to allow the enemy into my thoughts and life. Vengeance lifted its ugly head one day when I thought I was doing OK with forgiveness. Any negative news about the offender is good news! We can think, "Oh, he deserves that!" It is a good job the Lord does not think that way when we do wrong.

When we can forgive we experience a release from being bound to that other person. The constant thoughts and things that bring the person to mind are no longer hurtful. That is because the Lord has stepped in and freed us from the power of the enemy. Luke 6 v 37 says: "Forgive and you will be forgiven." You see if we do not forgive, the bible tells us that the Lord will not forgive us. For me forgiving has been a process when the more I drew nearer to the Lord the more I knew I had to forgive. I wanted to forgive because the Lord means more to me than obeying the enemy.

The enemy tries to tell us that it will be hard. Actually, once the decision is made in our minds and hearts, it is not hard at all and the relief and freedom we receive, and the peace which the Lord gives, is wonderful.

The year 2006 arrived and I was living on my own in the house which had been our family home. It was time to make changes. The next years still brought times of difficulty but the ongoing process of forgiving gets easier as we go along and see how the Lord blesses, not only me but it begins a chain of forgiveness in others too. Really believing, I have been restored and set free to minister to others.

I have learnt so much over these past years. My husband married again shortly after and has two children. I have grown in my faith. I love the Lord because He first loved me.

I am grateful that even when we make mistakes and go the wrong way the Lord in His wonderful mercy and forgiveness can make even the worst situation be used for His glory and not allow the enemy to win. The battle was won when Jesus died on the cross and gained victory over the enemy.

When my story began it was about the war years and I firmly believe that, right from the start, the Lord trained me for the future and enabled me to trust Him, and He has never failed me. Now my desire is that this experience will be of use, to minister to others who may have to go through the same or similar situation as I have.

Divorce is not the end. It is the beginning of a special walk with the Lord. If your conscience has pricked you while reading this part about forgiveness please take time and forgive that situation, person, incident, enemy, and the one who caused you so much pain, and perhaps still is, because if you have not forgiven you are not free.

It takes few words, and your conscious will, just to say: "I forgive because Jesus forgave me."

++++

Chapter 16 - Conclusions

In the last interview I had with the WEC in England, they advised me to make new friends, so I prayed for friends. One day shortly after this, back in Colombia and living in Bogotá, a missionary friend invited me to go with her to a women's bible study group. To my amazement, they were mostly American, but all spoke English. Now I could speak my own language and express myself so much better. They were a group of wives whose husbands were in Bogotá on business and often they were only in a country for a short time so did not know the language, and had no Christian help. We met on Wednesdays, and first we had a time of bible study, then prayer and later we had lunch together. What a banquet all this was for me and on top of it all they were so generous - each week my children enjoyed so many wonderful things to eat, because the ladies always gave me what was left from the meal to take home for the family.

In that group I met my special friend Cindy Pereira who is the only one left here in Bogotá – she is married to a Colombian and we still meet up now and then. With these dear women I learnt where my guilt feelings were coming from and how to deal with them.

Romans 8 verse 1 says "There is now no condemnation for those who are in Christ Jesus, who do not live according to the sinful nature but according to the spirit". I began to reject the lies and thank the Lord for his forgiving love to me.

When I look back over those dark times and my breakdown I have realised that it was caused by a list of multiple circumstances and now after many years I find that my experience can help others to see that the Lord healed me and can heal others through my testimony. The Lord can turn the enemy's attacks into blessings.

My four children have also lived their own battles but today I am so proud of each one of them. They have all achieved so much in their own situations - through their own determination and will to get on in life.

Yes, there are marks from the things they have had to live through, the constant packing and unpacking as we had to move so many different times – I lost count after about fifteen. Then there were the fearful situations with the guerrillas and the neighbours – sometimes the children threw stones at my son as he came home from school. We also had to face sickness too, when our only help was through prayer. But maybe the most difficult was now the shame of a father who has gone astray. Life is far from easy but I pray that each one of my dear children will continue to keep going as I have done.

****

<u>Editor's Note</u>

I have known Janet and her family from the mid-1980s, when my wife (Jan) and I moved to Leigh-on-Sea and started attending Leigh Road Baptist Church where, for many years, I was Missionary Secretary. We were also very pleased to be able to visit Janet in both Colombia and Switzerland.

When it became known that Janet had written a book in Spanish about her missionary life, many people started to encourage her to translate it into English. She was aware that, having spoken more Spanish than English for the last 40 years, the text in English would require some "polishing" and I feel privileged that she asked me to help edit her translation to achieve this.

This book does not follow the Spanish version exactly, as Janet made some changes as she translated it. In editing her English version, I have tried to remain as close to her translation as possible, so the style remains Janet's not mine. The main amendments have been to put the word order of sentences into a more usual form for English (Spanish word order is different), to remove a few duplications that had crept in and, as far as possible, to check on the chronological order of events that took place. I have worked closely with the family to achieve the final version.

One of the areas that I tried to encourage Janet to expand was to provide more details about circumstances that ultimately led to her divorce from Samuel. She was initially reluctant to do this, but did subsequently see the need for more information to be included. She had started some work on this, in the weeks before she finally went into hospital and subsequently went to be with the Lord, but little was found.

However, I believe we still have a very sound record of Janet's life, preparing for and subsequently going to the mission field – a life in which she constantly had to seek God's help and guidance.

Her hope was that this book would be, as well as a record of God's gracious dealings towards her, an encouragement and challenge to all who read it – may God bless you as you read it.

For me, it has been a joy and a blessing to know Janet, and her family.

Bob Hadwen.

1. Janet with Grandad (William Spillet)

2. Janet with sister Kath

3. School of Missionary Medicine

4. Wedding Day – 11th July 1970

5. Wedding Day – the Wedding Group!

6. Janet, Samuel, Samuel Jr and Miriam

7. Samuel Jr with Suzanne, plus Miriam and Martha

8. The Church at Yacopi (1975)

9. Early days of Mission Travel in Colombia!

10. River crossing – mission-style!

11. Church building.

12. Samuel baptising a believer.

13. The Church at Cedritos

14. The Church at Parque la Floresta

15. Sami, Miriam, Martha and Suzanne – Switzerland 2002

16. Sami, Miriam, Martha and Suzanne – Switzerland 2002